The goal of pai

Nicolas Poussin

There are no dogmas about inspiration
except that it is required for work of the highest value.

Adam Phillips, psychoanalyst and writer (Going Sane)

National status is increasingly defined by culture.

Roger Hilton

My wish is that we might lose our confidence in what we
think we believe
and the things we consider stable and secure,
in order to remind ourselves
of the infinite number of things waiting to be discovered.

Anton Tapies, Catalan artist

Ardwyn Lewis, my father

NO MOD CONS

No Mod Cons

Mary Lloyd Jones

ISBN: 978-1-84524-228-2

Cover design: Mary Lloyd Jones/Eleri Owen

Published by Gwasg Carreg Gwalch,
12 Iard yr Orsaf, Llanrwst, Wales LL26 0EH
tel: 01492 642031
fax: 01492 641502
email: books@carreg-gwalch.com
internet: www.carreg-gwalch.com

Contents

Foreword

It's nearly fifty years since my wife and I saw several of the colourful Ceredigion landscapes which the young Mary Lloyd Jones was then painting. Thrilled by the possibility of owning one, we invited ourselves to visit her studio. Somewhat chastened, we discovered that she had recently abandoned her early style in favour of we perceived as abstraction, though Mary might describe it as a more profound kind of representation. Fortunately for us, one picture from that early period remained, of Aber-arth. We bought it, and love it still for its rich colours. Four decades later, when Mary and John came to lunch, she stood stunned: 'Whose work is that?' she asked, and was delighted by the answer.

It's painful to recall how backward, sixty years ago, was the public presence of the fine arts in Wales. There was the National Museum in Cardiff, the Glynn Vivian in Swansea, the National Library (restrained in exhibiting, but collecting invaluably), the National Eisteddfod for one week a year, but little else. Yet even in this dry land artists were hard at work, both immigrants and residents, especially those whose work was bought by Winifred Coombe Tennant, a remarkable woman in a world of men.

Yet women, struggling against all the age-old prejudices, began to emerge. One can hardly count the wonderful Gwen John, so much a project of Paris and London. Their leaders in Wales have been a lonely Brenda Chamberlain, followed by Mary Lloyd Jones and Claudia Williams: many more have emerged since. In this book Mary gives a lively account of her struggles both to paint on her own account and to organise a better world for Welsh artists.

Mary's presence in Aberystwyth, in Ceredigion and in Wales, is an ongoing delight – and a challenge too. Her elfin smile, her zest for life, her pioneering spirit are as bright as ever. She was the first person I heard suggesting that the splendid Old College building, from which all academic life had migrated up Penglais hill, would make an excellent national centre for the arts in Wales. Her vision won't be accomplished easily, but Mary sees difficulties as challenges, and she is now the first artist in residence there. *Hir oes a llwyddiant* – long life and success!

Gerald Morgan
Aberystwyth, 2014

Me as a toddler

Boarding the narrow gauge railway train for Devil's Bridge

Introduction

Reflecting that I have spent six decades focusing on becoming an artist, forging a visual expression on the foundation of a rural childhood – mapping the steps that led to my present situation – might, I thought, be an interesting project. The stark contrast that exists between my childhood in the 1930s and 40s in Devil's Bridge (*Pontarfynach*), Ceredigion, and the present turbulent and unsettled times, where global catastrophies are a constant backdrop even in the remotest communities, is the theme of these writings.

Whilst the hills, fields, gorges and precipices, the physical features of the landscape of my childhood, remain, the pattern of living has changed completely, and I now realise that I was privileged to have a truly rural experience in early childhood. I have learned that that something in the region of 50 per cent of the world's population now lives in an urban environment. The acute disadvantages (as I perceived them) related to life in Devil's Bridge during the Second World War have been transformed, with advancing years, into a rare and valued experience.

Mary Lloyd Jones
Aberystwyth, summer 2014

Rhiwmynach

The cowshed was a lean-to zinc shed attached to the back of the stone cottage. Further zinc extensions accommodated a hay shed, coal shed and chicken house and a pigsty. The heady smells of fresh dung and musty hay, and the disorder of ancient discarded objects, were a constant feature of my childhood.

Mysterious and unexpected was the presence of a gilded, full-size concert harp resting on the beams above the cows. It transpired that this harp had been played by my father's brother Dai, who was killed in the First World War. My father and his brother had walked to give performances in neighbouring villages with the harp strapped on their backs. These concerts were never mentioned, no doubt the

William Arthur Lewis (Willy), my father's oldest brother, who died at twenty-four from pneumonia

very existence of the harp brought back memories which were too painful. So this exotic object, glinting gold underneath the cobwebs, seems surprising only when viewed in retrospect after the passage of years.

The death in their early twenties of my father's three older brothers cast a long shadow over relationships within the family. The eldest brother, Willy, a brilliant scholar amongst the first generations of students at Aberystwyth University, died at the age of twenty-four within three days of contracting pneumonia. The books he won

Dai, who went with my father to perform in nearby villages; after Dai's death in the First World War his gilded harp was lodged on the beams in the cowshed

Emrys, my father's third brother, who also died in the War

as school prizes, still in my possession, and my father's tales of his talent as a maker of toys to amuse his younger siblings, are reminders of the loss. Emrys, also a graduate of Aberystwyth University, and Dai, the singer and harpist, were both killed in the 1914–18 war. I have come to realise that these tragic events were to affect the character of my father and to shape events and relationships within the family until the death of my parents and brother.

My father's fourth and youngest brother was an invalid who lived with us. His regular suffering of breathless attacks, unalleviated in those days by inhalers or drugs, was caused by damaged heart valves. It was a constant background to my childhood. Unable to work or walk far he spent his days sitting and reading. When all reading material was exhausted

Uncle Phillip, the youngest brother, wearing the postman's hat

My grandfather, Jenkin Lewis, returning from chapel – the Rhiwmynach petrol pump is in the background

his hunger for the printed word left him reading the dictionary. From him I caught the reading bug, and received much encouragement with all my interests. He was a fervent supporter of Plaid Cymru and my first conversations about politics were with him. Daily and weekly newspapers came to Rhiwmynach, including the leading Welsh political publications, *Y Cymro*, *Y Faner* and, for my brother and myself, *Cymru'r Plant*.

A very early memory is of myself standing in the kitchen dwarfed by a forest of chair legs, the chairs themselves supporting layers of ironed sheets and shirts. A hazy figure lurks behind the hanging washing, and this I take to be my grandfather, a benevolent presence behind a newspaper – a kindly bearded gentleman, but the memory is not precise. My grandfather died when I was two.

Another very early memory is being taken by my father to visit 'Y Ffatri'. My father and grandfather were weavers, with a small woollen mill situated by the narrow gauge railway line in

Devil's Bridge. They wove *carthenni* [blankets] and spun wool for women to knit into socks. The depression in the thirties killed this business; they stopped weaving in 1936 when I was two. I remember distinctly the characteristic oily smell of the cones of wool, and picking up trailing ends of greasy yarn and the old cones that were lying on the floor. The colours of the yarns were subdued dark reds, grey and black and the whole building had an air of silent decay, which was, at the same time, rather strange and mysterious. The slate floor finished suddenly, confronting one with a yawning hole where one could see into the cavernous basement. Outside, rushing water turned the mill wheel and the whole building balanced above a precipitous drop of several hundred feet down to the Rheidol river far below.

It is only now that I can fully appreciate how my early experiences in this remarkable environment must have had a profound influence on my imagination. Devil's Bridge is a scattered settlement situated where the river Mynach joins the Rheidol, cascading over a steep gorge to form the Mynach Falls. These steep-sided valleys, full of mysterious shadows and dramatic silhouettes, were to me the normal world. This world was also dangerous. Almost every year there were accidents. People fell from trees or slipped on wet rocks and fell to their deaths. I remember as a small child peering through the bridge over the gorge at the swirling black water far below. The association with the Devil could not have been without some influence. It must have impressed on me that there was a dark and dangerous side to the natural world. Many places, of course, were forbidden to us as children, but as I grew older and more adventurous these steep-sided hillsides, precipitous rocks and slippery paths were fully explored. I could say that at one time I knew every tree, every rock, every hidden cranny, all the flora in an area of several square miles. This

My mother and me

familiarity with a particular place and the awareness of changing seasons has provided me with a store of images which are the foundation of my paintings.

During the thirties, Devil's Bridge was already an area that was suffering from depopulation. After the decline of the lead mining industry men had had to leave the area to obtain work in the coalfields of south Wales. In a sparsely-populated countryside my childhood was therefore fairly isolated. School friends would live several miles away, so I was forced to create my own amusement for much of the time. There was very little money for toys and during the war shortages of all kinds were normal. The result was that I made most of my own dolls. I had always an almost frantic need to make things. I was forever pleading with my mother to cut up perfectly sound and useful articles so that I could make from them objects of my own design. These were usually dolls, or bags, fully lined and embroidered. Another passion was for cutting out figures from my mother's mail order catalogues and using the characters in theatrical situations of make-believe. In a rural area shopping for clothes was often by mail order. The arrival of a new catalogue from Oxendales, Pontings, Price Jones or Daniel Neal was an occasion of great excitement for me. Unfortunately for my poor mother I would want to cut these up almost immediately; looking back, keeping me satisfied with materials to cut up must have been very trying for her.

My mother was not interested in sewing, so my enthusiasm for this activity did not grow from watching her. What I recall of her during my early years is as someone who always had too much to do. The horror of washing day is firmly implanted on my mind: the zinc bath with billowing suds, the washboard, and the endless array of wet clothes. The steam and wetness continued for the whole day and ended only in late afternoon when my mother used the last of the water to wash the floor. My mother's wrinkled red hands and her imprisonment in the round of domestic labour impressed on me the need to concentrate on finding another way to survive.

Although often tired and overworked my mother had a romantic streak in her personality and often showed a keen response to the weather, the seasons, flowers and bird life. Her tendency to collect catalogues and to send for things by post led to her acquiring a catalogue of Medici prints. In this catalogue I saw my first reproductions of the work of Italian Renaissance painters. The paintings by Raphael and Botticelli were only postage-stamp size, but held a total fascination for me.

My father's family were great readers. A prominent piece of furniture in Rhiwmynach was the bookcase. Each year a scheme supported by the local authority existed to encourage the purchase of Welsh books. The catalogue for this project was eagerly awaited, and its arrival was the beginning of a period of intense discussion. My parents and Uncle Phillip made their choices and my brother and I were encouraged to choose one book each. This in a household where money was in very short supply; nevertheless, a budget for books was added to sums already spent on newspapers and periodicals. The bookcase stored many of my grandfather's books, many on Biblical themes, which I found less attractive. Of more interest were two leather-bound tomes, one written in Welsh, *Hanes y Brytaniaid a'r Cymry* [the history of the British and the Welsh], and dated 1870, by Gweirydd ap Rhys, and a pictorial edition of the *Life and Discoveries of David Livingstone*, dated 1889, both signed on the frontispiece by Jenkin Lewis, my grandfather. Gweirydd ap Rhys was by profession a weaver who had had no formal schooling, but who had taught himself to read by propping a book on his loom. No doubt, for my grandfather he was a hero.

My parents bought a set of ten volumes of *Arthur Mee's Children's Encyclopaedia*. This treasure provided me with an introduction to many fields and showed me glimpses of a vast world that I could explore. I tackled the heavy tomes by trying out my reading skills, first on illustrated nursery rhymes. Guided by Uncle Phillip I moved on to stories from different cultures and as my understanding developed I could read about history, geography, science and engineering, although these subjects were less attractive than the history of painting. I was evidently attracted by colour from an early age and my favourite pages in the enclopaedia were colour pages on the natural world, collections of botanical paintings, fish of all kinds, underwater plants, shells, fossils, geological samples and collections of minerals. I returned time and again to the pages of wild flowers and copying line drawings on to pieces of cotton, which I would then attempt to embroider.

I cannot place too much value on the doors which were opened to me through these pages. The lives of explorers, inventors, writers, artists and scientists were paraded before my imagination. Nearly all these potential role models were, of course, men, although this did not occur to me at the time. Nevertheless, I was puzzled by the fact that in the atlas section all the English counties were shown, but nowhere could the counties of Wales be seen. But the encyclopaedia was an introduction to subjects like Greek mythology and astronomy, and it was in this way that I gained a smattering of information about many fields.

Like virtually all the inhabitants of Devil's Bridge in the thirties my father was a tenant of the Hafod estate, renting the cottage and approximately 7 acres, which could support three cows. Another lean-to structure was attached to the house, and was called '*y bac*' [the back]. This was where the produce of the smallholding was processed to become food for the table. This building housed a stone structure which could accommodate a fire underneath a cauldron for boiling clothes. Next to this stood a churn and in an outer section a large table where my mother's father (a butcher) could salt the sides of bacon before storage in a tea chest. These eventually became sides of bacon which hung from the ceiling of this multipurpose room. Another piece of equipment was the separator, a small machine turned by hand, which separated the cream from the milk in readiness for butter-making. Turning the handle of the separator was the task of my brother and myself.

The startling changes that have occurred during my

lifetime can be viewed clearly when the processes that I have described are considered in relation to the antiseptic Disneyland experience of collecting food from the supermarket. My parents and grandparents practiced self-sufficiency; my first-hand experience of this left me bemused about, if sympathetic to, the invasion of self-sufficiency enthusiasts to west Wales in the 1960s.

The cow was central to survival on the small income of a council roadman. My mother made butter; we had a plentiful supply of milk and sold the surplus to a few neighbours who arrived to collect it in enamel cans. The skimmed milk from the separator was fed to the pig. All waste trimmings from vegetables were fed to the pig, who was a most efficient recycling machine. Owning three cows entailed harvesting hay for winter feed and walking the cows from the fields in time for milking. I must admit that I was pressured into walking the cows home. To me at the time this was an embarrassment, as en route home I would encounter tourists, who, to my eyes, seemed from another planet. In contrast, to them my status as a peasant child was unambiguous.

Slaughtering the animals for food and the messy process of them giving birth was the backdrop to my childhood. To view the slaughtered pig hanging vertically ready for the removal of the entrails was shocking; even worse were the screams before the knife reached the jugular. Viewing the bloody afterbirth after the arrival of a new calf in the night one experienced wonder and disgust in equal measure.

Sides of bacon hanging from the ceiling create a wholesome image of healthy plentiful food. The truth is that I never enjoyed eating home-cured bacon as the amount of fat was more than my digestion could handle. When the pig was newly slaughtered my mother made brawn from the pig's head, adding a lot of pepper. This was considered a delicacy, but here also the high proportion of fat gave me problems.

Chickens were killed by chopping their heads off, and I recall my mother plucking the feathers and gutting the bird to reveal small eggs minus the shells, a piece of domestic theatre that was in no way extraordinary at the time. Self-sufficiency included breadmaking in a large earthenware crock. The rising dough seemed magical. My brother and I were allowed to play with a small portion of dough, creating strangely-shaped rather grubby lumps of bread which, once baked, we could eat ... a creative exercise which was missing in our school curriculum.

The rather unkempt garden produced potatoes, carrots, shallots, cabbage and lettuce with a flavour not experienced since. Many blackcurrant and redcurrant bushes gave the most intense flavour I have ever tasted. I was much praised when during one of my mother's rare absences I succeeded in making some blackcurrant tarts at about the age of seven.

The privy (or '*tŷ bach*': *tŷ* = house, *bach* = little) was one end of the garden, built over a stream which flooded periodically, providing a naturally-induced flush. Could it be that the product of the *tŷ bach* contributed to the excellent quality of the blackcurrants? I can recall little weeding being done and nettles flourished in the undisturbed corners. Young nettle leaves were cooked periodically, producing a excellent green vegetable of good flavour to add further variety to the diet.

In addition to the garden produce certain wild fruits were seasonally collected. Blackberries, of course, but also whinberries (*llus duon bach*) found in the hedges and on the upland moorlands. With my visiting cousins and aunts, expeditions to collect whinberries were arranged so that whinberry tarts could be enjoyed. We children enjoyed threading the whinberries on to long grasses and then eating the berries in large flavourful mouthfuls that left lips and teeth stained navy blue. The virulent but delicious stains would creep on to hands and clothes, which annoyed the mothers.

Beryl Lewis, my mother, and her brother, ny Uncle Islwyn (1952)

My first drawings were of people, members of my family, and from the beginning it seems that they took an interest in my activity and gave me encouragement. I enjoyed the praise I received for my ability to achieve a recognisable likeness. So I continued along this path. When I was seven I remember the teacher asking us in school what we would like to be, and I distinctly remember thinking that I wanted to be an artist. I was too embarrassed to admit this, however, and felt the other children might laugh, so I said I wanted to be a waitress, or something of the sort.

When I was a little older it occurred to me that proper

artists sat outside and painted from the landscape, so I thought I might try to do this. I doubt if I would have taken this step had I not been certain that no one would see me. I was not surrounded by other children, who might have thought that sitting down to paint a landscape was an odd activity for a nine- or ten-year-old. I was able to experiment with drawing and painting in a way that would not have been possible in an urban thickly-populated environment.

My mother playing the piano (1952)

Every Saturday, from the age of eight until I went to grammar school in Aberystwyth at the age of eleven, I used to walk about two miles to receive a piano lesson, a round trip of about four miles, but this was not considered exceptional in any way. Very few villagers had cars and it was quite normal to walk three or four miles to visit the cobbler, the tailor, to attend an Eisteddfod or to go to a concert.

My journeys for piano lessons have imprinted themselves on my mind permanently as tests of endurance.

At this time I was terrified of any strange dogs (I still have a considerable fear of dogs). On my trips for the piano lesson I had to pass three houses that had noisy, aggressive dogs. As I approached each house my fear would build up and I would pass the house with pounding heart and dry mouth. I was never bitten and I never told my parents of my fear, but the fact remains that every Saturday contained six endurance tests without counting the actual piano lesson. During the winter months dusk would begin to fall during my journey home and my heightened senses saw strange figures hiding behind the bushes; no sooner was one hazard passed than another would be perceived. My habit of creating shapes from elements in the landscape perhaps stems from from heightened awareness born of fear experienced at this time. The will required to pass fierce dogs six times every Saturday for three years has probably been a good training in perseverance that has enabled me to continue painting in spite of difficulties to this day.

I remember my piano teacher's house with some pleasure. Reaching it in one piece was of course a great relief, but I remember most being intrigued by the colourful rag mats scattered over the highly-polished flagstone floor.

For a child, haymaking was great fun. For adults concerned to get a good crop under cover in erratic weather it must have been a time of stress and anxiety. What I remember is the smell of newly-mown fields and the excitement of leapfrogging over the 'mydylau', pyramids of hay, with my cousins who came to stay with my grandparents in the summer holidays. These gymnastics infuriated my grandfather. The high spot of a haymaking day was being allowed to ride on the horse-drawn load into the hay shed.

My father enjoyed tinkering with engineering projects, attempting to move with the times. One project was cutting

Haymaking at Penlonfedw (1949)

a car in half and constructing a platform for carrying hay where the back seat had been. This cobbled-together vehicle was a great embarrassment for me. But my brother had hours of pleasure driving it in the field adjoining our house, and it enabled him to learn to drive when he was perhaps only nine or ten. The area around the house could not be called manicured and a level of disorder was normal. Anything that was broken was thrown into the garden hedge, so while my brother played with the car/lorry I would find bits of broken china and old bottles and with these create an imaginary world.

At this time, the period after the war, I can recall something which is never heard in a rural village these days – the sound of footsteps. Groups of people would pass our house along the tarmac road to attend concerts and plays in what was called Tyn Llwyn. This was a bungalow structure built especially to serve the tourists during the season as a tea shop (it is still there, at the entrance to the caravan park on the Ponterwyd side of the bridge). During the winter months it would be transformed into a makeshift theatre by creating a stage at one end from all the tables pushed together, with a flimsy curtain strung across on a wire emulating a theatre curtain. This arrangement had to be refreshed at the beginning of the winter season, and I recall my mother rushing off, a roll of paper under her arm, to hang fresh wallpaper on the set. Performers from neighbouring villages – and sometimes from as far afield as Llanelli – would perform thrilling one, two, or three-act plays, or present concert programmes of solos, duets or recitations. I can even remember a conjuror and a dancer who performed on the rickety table tops, which must have been quite dangerous and would be impossible in today's regime of Health and Safety. These proceedings were always in Welsh, and were the high spots of my life during the dark nights of winter. In order to attend these events, walking by torchlight was necessary; there were no street lights. Very few people had cars, so parking was never a problem. Tickets for these events would be sold during the preceding weeks and the profits invariably went towards maintaining a chapel, either in Pontarfynach or in one of the neighbouring villages. The Bungalow, in spite of its shortcomings, was considered superior to a school or chapel in Trisant, Ystumtuen, or Cwmystwyth for performances that would attract a sizeable audience of 150-200. Pontarfynach – I have now, as I write, realised – was a community focal point for an area with a radius of eight to ten miles.

There were other reasons for venturing out after dark on winter nights. *Yr Aelwyd*, a branch of the *Urdd Gobaith Cymru* (Welsh League of Youth) was held once a week in the primary school. My father, with his friends, was involved in drawing up a programme for the *Aelwyd*. This would consist of quizzes, debates, storytelling – all conducted with

My father, Ardwyn Lewis, in front of Rhiwmynach

much humour and leg-pulling. Sometimes there was a guest speaker. For some reason, my mother was always responsible for refreshments, an important part of the proceedings, so each *Aelwyd* night there was the preliminary task of making enough paste sandwiches for twenty or thirty people.

Aelwyd nights were an impressive example of working social glue. These nights were invariably fun, with lots of laughter, unpretentious, accommodating all ages from ten to eighty, and generated a huge credit of goodwill and social support. Rural communities in Wales functioned as supportive structures many centuries before David Cameron was moved to promote his Big Society. I realise that the civilised and caring society – *Brawdoliaeth War* – celebrated by the poet Waldo Williams with such distinction was part of my everyday experience during my formative years. Neighbours helped each other when many hands were needed for harvesting the hay, and sheep-shearing involved large gatherings of hill farmers, helping each other in hard physical work in an atmosphere of feasting and celebration, with much leg-pulling and laughter. When a family in Pontarfynach lost a cow, neighbours collected enough money to buy a replacement. Everyone who took part in these sociabilities spoke *Cymraeg*. *Cymraeg* was the unquestioned norm.

The extramural classes run by the university in Aberystwyth were an important feature of life for my father and his brother. These were held by distinguished scholars; Sir Ifan ab Owen Edwards (his father Sir Owen M. Edwards established 'Urdd Gobaith Cymru' The Welsh League of Youth, both father and son spent their lives promoting the Welsh language) ran a series of classes on (I believe) Welsh history. Some years the subject might be a branch of science. A copy of *The Mabinogi* in Old Welsh now in my possession was a course book for one of these classes. For those like my father and his brother who had not had an opportunity for an education beyond the age of twelve, these classes were a lifeline, opening the doors to a wider world, and helping to provide some food to alleviate the hunger for learning that was a family characteristic. Rhiwmynach had four volumes of *The World's Great Books*, edited by Arthur Mee and S. A. Hammerton, inscribed in 1910 by D. D. Lewis, my father's

Auntie Meg (1948)

Uncle Phillip (1948)

brother, the harpist who later died in the war. Uncle Phillip showed me the story of *Alice in Wonderland* in Volume Two. These books housed an impressive array of world classics from all cultures. Further evidence of my father and his brothers' search for education were a few pages from *The Popular Educator*, found at the back of a cupboard, date unknown but containing chapters on Chemistry, Greek, Sketching from Nature, French, Applied Mathematics, and Algebra.

The material investigated in the extra-mural classes was undoubtedly challenging. I recently found *Detholiad o'r Hen Gyfreithiau Cymraeg o Amser Hywel Dda* – a text book on the old Welsh laws of Hywel Dda (d. 950: a prince who ruled most of Wales; his laws were used for several hundreds of years in Wales) with an introduction by the Welsh scholar Sir John Lloyd, published in 1938, which belonged to my father. With no distraction from television, time spent listening to inspired lectures in small rooms lit by oil lamps can be viewed as a stark contrast to the diet of reality TV and the general dumbing-down of popular culture that we have today.

Dumfriesshire to Eisteddfa Gurig, 1650

In my family, the story is told of how Lewis McMazon, in the mid eighteenth century embarked on a journey to Wales with a relative named Richard Cox, from Dumfriesshire. John Peel, a young man who had lived for a time in south Wales, persuaded them to set out with him, with sheep, goats and horses for the hills of Cardiganshire. They reached Eisteddfa Gurig on the southern side of Pumlumon and immediately set to work to build themselves a hut and a sheep fold. They were not welcomed by the local farming community, who treated them to every kind of insult; they were called thieves and robbers, and the people tried to frighten them away – in desperation, calling in a wizard from Radnorshire to pronounce a curse on the strangers, which would bring harm to anyone to anyone who traded with them.

As a result Lewis and Richard were obliged to go for provisions to the next county, to Machynlleth, and it fell to the lot of John Peel, who knew Welsh, to do their commissions.

The strangers had with them three dogs, who attracted a lot of attention in the county. Their names were Alex, Tic and Mas. It was thought that these were the prototypes of the silver-eyed sheepdogs that became so prevalent in these parts. The names, in any case, persisted, and many dogs were named after them. The strangers were fortunate to find a protector in Shami Sion Shami, the owner of Aberpeithnant. This man, who towered head and shoulders above his neighbours, forbade them to do the strangers any harm. Towards the month of October John, Lewis and Richard moved away, to the delight of the natives, who thought they had got rid of them.

The next May, however, they appeared again with more sheep. What they did at this period was to spend the summer months in Wales and then in October go to sell their sheep in England. At the end of each October they would buy Scottish sheep to take back with them to Cardiganshire.

John Peel had nothing to do with the animals, but one day, three years after he, Richard and Lewis had arrived in these parts, he went to Machynlleth as usual, and on the way back he was taken ill with a mortal sickness, the result (so Lewis thought) of drinking sour beer. In agony, John called in at a farm called Cefn Coch and asked if he might lie on the straw with the animals. Alas, the farmers turned a deaf ear, and he was left to die on the road.

It happened that it was Machynlleth Fair day. Shami Sion Shami's two daughters had attended the fair, and were riding home when they came upon John's body. They decided to go to tell his friends Lewis and Richard, but were at a loss to know how to proceed, because they were sure the men didn't speak a word of Welsh. They went anyway, and found, to their surprise, that they did speak Welsh tolerably well, having learned it from John Peel.

Thus began a secret courtship.

John Peel was buried in Penygoes churchyard. While his friends were at the funeral, their enemies seized the opportunity to kill and carry off their sheep. They were hauled before the authorities in Cardiganshire, but released thanks to Shami Sion Shami, who went to court and testified that they had been taking away their own sheep, not stealing; the sheep in question were a different breed to Lewis and Richard's.

Some time after this, Shami Sion Shami's two daughters disappeared, and could not be found. Nobody knows to this day where they went! When they returned, they were married to Richard Cox and Lewis Mac Mazon. Their father was furious, and never forgave them.

Elizabeth began her married life in a shanty that her husband Lewis had put up for them in the hills on the way to Machynlleth, where the farm of Gwenffrwd now stands. Lewis was a good craftsman, and made various pieces of furniture, some of which survives to this day.

My great-great-grandfather Lewis Mason of Llerneuaddau, the son of the original Lewis Mac Mazon, was the brother of John Mason of Creignant Bach. Jane Mason, daughter of John Mason, married Huw Rees; their son was Sir John Rhys, Oxford scholar and leading Welsh academic.

Dafydd Jones, the Master Shipbuilder

Whilst writing this account, looking up family documents, discovering details about my great-great-grandfather has been a positive experience. It has helped me to understand my need as a child to be constantly making and drawing. Until now, it seemed that no one else in my family had the same obsession, not among my contemporaries or in previous generations – until I learnt the story of this remarkable man. It has been an extraordinary comfort to realise that certain characteristics can skip generations and emerge again in different form when opportunities are available.

The following information about Dafydd Jones is taken from an article by R. Gareth Owen.

Dafydd Jones was born in Llanddewi, Aberarth, a busy little port. Many of his relations were connected with seafaring in some way. One of the most prominent was his uncle, Evan Jones. Already, by the standards of the time, Evan was a wealthy and prosperous man, with his own shipbuilding yard. The fact that he could go to 'take the waters' at Llandrindod Wells was an indication of his success. When Dafydd came of age, he was naturally apprenticed to his uncle, at 11s a week.

However, in June 1845 disaster struck. Evan had decided to go to 'take the waters' and had left his young nephew to supervise the building of the *Adroit*, which was on the stocks in the yard. Suddenly there was a cloudburst, the like of which Aberarth had never seen. Everything was swept away by floodwater, and when Evan returned he was close to being a ruined man.

But young Dafydd had the sense and vision to move to Aberaeron, which was booming following the building of the new harbour in 1807. With the urge to be his own master, and with the prospect of prosperity, he and his uncle had the *Adroit* towed to Aberaeron harbour.

Even though he was young, Dafydd Jones emerged as a shipbuilder of high repute and natural brilliance. He helped other shipbuilders in the town, giving them work rigging ships – a bill for forty-nine days' labour is recorded at 26s a day. He built a family home, Neptune House. He had a flair for modern techniques. He could convert a ketch or sloop into a schooner by cutting the hull amidships and inserting a new portion to lengthen the ship. He built his ships for speed; one of the fastest was *Pleiades*, a schooner built in 1866.

He was mathematically brilliant. He had not had any formal schooling, but his ability to calculate trigonometrical and other mathematical problems was well known. He could calculate in his head the rigging requirements of a vessel from a wooden half-model made to scale. After his death, a national newspaper said:

> David Jones, a shipbuilder from Aberaeron, although without mathematical training could calculate mentally draught tonnage and rigging for his ships.

Dafydd's reputation spread far and wide; although he had not been to sea himself his skill was known to many, from Shanghai to Bordeaux. As the schooner industry declined, Dafydd carried out repairs for various ship owners. He would leave Aberaeron for Newport or Cardiff with an army of sixty workmen to repair a barque in dry dock in one of the larger ports.

While trying to learn more about Dafydd Jones, I discovered that the *Cadwgan*, the last ship built by him, sailed from Aberaeron on 1 February 1888 carrying republican sympathisers to Wicklow in Ireland; they arrived in Wicklow on 5 February after a difficult crossing, and from there they went by train to Dublin, where they met with Tom Ellis MP.

Dafydd Jones was a capable administrator. He employed eighty to 100 men at his yard, and it was he who first introduced scheduled working hours, as opposed to a morning and a night shift.

When his yard was empty he went into retirement – but not for long. He decided to try being a ship-owner as well as a builder. He bought a magnificent three-masted barque, the *Madras*, and for a few years traded all round the world. But on 10 March 1891 the *Madras* foundered with all hands in a squall in the Bristol Channel. Newspapers carried headlines of 'Aberaeron in its mourning', for practically every house was in mourning. Dafydd Jones himself lost two sons in this tragedy: Evan, who was the captain, and Jenkin, mate, and under them was a crew made up of local youths and seamen.

Dafydd Jones had married Grace Jones in 1822. As well as Evan and Jenkin, they had a daughter, born in 1828, also named Grace.

Mary Anne, my grandmother, was born to Grace in 1856. On her birth certificate, the mother's name is recorded as Grace Jones, but the father's name is not included. When Mary Anne was five, Grace, her mother, married David Davies, a relieving officer from Llanarth.

The discovery that Mary Anne, my grandmother, was illegitimate came as a surprise; this fact was not known to my parents or to any other members of the family. Knowing the attitude of a chapel-dominated culture towards a 'fallen woman', the difficulties that must have been endured by my grandmother and great-grandmother add a tragic note to this secret family history.

I consider that the success and status enjoyed in the community by Dafydd Jones was an important factor in finding a husband for Grace.

Mary Anne died before I was born, and endured the loss of three sons, who must have inherited some of the brilliance of Dafydd Jones, but were savagely cut down in their early twenties.

Jenkin Lewis and Mary Anne;
back, Dilys Lewis; centre, next to Mary Ann – Ardwyn Lewis;
standing, Phillip

Ysgol Mynach

My first experience of primary school in September 1939 must have coincided with the outbreak of the Second World War. A ditch had been created in the playground with a deep and shallow end designed to serve as an air raid shelter. At the signal of a special whistle blown by the headmaster we were trained to run into the shelter, big children at the deep end and graded according to size to the shallow end. As perhaps the smallest child in the school my place was last in at the shallow end, and crouching underneath an arrangement of branches designed as camouflage. The wartime regime involved gas mask drill and practice in decoding the pattern of whistles: short whistles meant danger from gas and a prolonged whistle indicated an approaching air raid. Devil's Bridge did not suffer an air raid but I do recall the family standing outside one night gazing at a red sky. 'Someone is getting it tonight', was the verdict. This was, in fact, one of the nights when Swansea was bombed. The war was a vague concept serving as a backdrop to the more pressing problem of learning to accept school. At home there was much serious talk with neighbours and family about '*y rhyfel*' [*rhyfel* = war]. But I had no idea of the meaning of this frequently-used word.

The technique of colonisation – the forerunner of empire-building – was first practised on '*Y Cymru*', the first people of *Prydain* [Britain] by Anglo-Saxon invaders. The most important part of the process of colonisation was to kill the language and debase the culture, Owen Edwards has a moving account in *Clych Atgof* (published in Caernarfon in 1906) of the immeasurable damage inflicted on Welsh children by the disciplinary system known as the Welsh Not. Whilst *Cymraeg* was the language of my home and that of all

38

members of the extended family and neighbours, much of the teaching in the school was in English.

I did not, however, suffer from the Welsh Not, as that barbaric practice had stopped in 1939, but scars still remain. In order to eliminate the use of Welsh as soon as possible a piece of wood on which the letters W and N were carved was attached to a piece of string. If a child was caught speaking Welsh (other children were encouraged to make this known), and the piece of wood was hung around the child's neck. The piece of wood travelled from one child to another throughout the day and the child wearing the Welsh Not at the end of the day received a caning. The system encouraged children to bully and tell tales, eliminating any instinct for loyalty amongst friends. Owen Edwards, in his biography, describes vividly the poisonous effect this horrific system had on his attitude towards education and the Welsh language. In spite of his unhappy early experiences he rose to be a national hero, an Oxford scholar, prolific author and an inspiration for generations of followers.

The four books that have been published about my work since 2001, and the fact that my work is included in the Welsh curriculum, have led to direct contact with many schools, both primary and secondary, and with teachers throughout Wales. This connection has been a most rewarding and satisfying development, contributing a whole new dimension to my life as an artist. The fact that today many children in Wales can experience the rewards of creative endeavour, and receive enthusiastic encouragement from some remarkable teachers, gives me hope for the future of a Welsh culture that embraces the visual arts with confidence. Here I will mention three teachers: Anne Davies in Llangybi school, and Daisy Prendergast and Cen Williams, and also the teachers at Ysgol Cefn Coch, Cardiff.

Unlike children today, who have sent me their paintings after looking at my books and films, the curriculum in 1939 as I recall it consisted of chanting multiplication tables and endless arithmetic problems about digging holes and calculating the speed of trains passing each other. The fare was bleak and uninspiring. We learnt nothing of history, about plant and bird life, no games or school visits and certainly no art.

There were no art materials, but I remember struggling with hand-sewing a pillow case (with much unpicking) and the boys could do raffia work on a Friday afternoon. It is a fact that I received more inspiration from *Arthur Mee's Children's Encyclopaedia* at home than I was given in the primary school. I reacted badly to the arithmetic lessons, but I acquired a reading skill with little difficulty. *Cymraeg* was the language of my home, and I first learnt to read in Welsh.

My brother David, sleeping (1952)

The Hafod Estate

In 1934, the year that I was born, the population of Wales was divided into landowners and tenants. In 2012 the aspiration of the majority to be able to own their own home has been dented by the tsunami of repossessions and bankruptcies that have followed the banking crisis that continues.

Rhiwmynach was a smallholding on the Hafod Estate with an annual rent of £8.00. In my possession is the catalogue of the sale of the Hafod Estate comprising farms, smallholdings and cottage properties, held in July 1947. The estate extended to about 3,413 acres, producing an annual rent of £2619 14s 6d. The quality of the land in this upland area was always poor; the large families and squalid cottages allowed tuberculosis to decimate the local population in a short period of time.

Nevertheless, Hafod mansion and the estate had brought fame and a place on the tourist route for those seeking a sublime landscape experience. The Estate was inherited by Thomas Johnes in 1783, and it was he who was responsible for expanding and improving the estate, as well as for planting woodlands. He was a patron of the Arts. Turner was a visitor, also Thomas Jones Pencerrig and John Warwick Smith produced many paintings and engravings of Hafod. Thomas also set up one of the earliest printing presses in Wales and was a pioneer of agriculture. Tragically, his famous library containing priceless Welsh manuscripts was destroyed by fire.

Whilst Thomas Johnes of Hafod possessed a vision and enthusiasm directed to improving the quality of life for his tenants and introducing the wonders of central Wales uplands to his cultured friends. But the record of the landowners of vast tracts of Wales is depressing. Wealth was squandered on gambling and irresponsible extravagance. The estates frequently changed hands due to mortgaging difficulties, creating constant instability whilst abandoning any support for the Welsh language and culture. Even Thomas Johnes' last days ended in bankruptcy.

Centuries before his time Johnes provided health care and free schools for his tenants. The seeds planted in Hafod over the years bore some fruit in the form of the love of books and learning which lingers in many peasant families of this part of Ceredigion, not least my own ancestors.

Rereading *Peacocks in Paradise* by Elizabeth Inglis Jones, an account of Hafod during the lifetime of Thomas Johnes, it is uncanny that one of my heroes, Iolo Morgannwg, was a frequent visitor to the Hafod Library. Iolo always travelled on foot. In attempting to build a Welsh visual language I have frequently borrowed the Bardic alphabet documented by Iolo as a way of embedding a Welsh identity in my paintings. A pattern of continuing connection appears as I think of myself following in Iolo's footsteps climbing that same road to Cwmystwyth and Hafod after an interval of more than 200 years.

A scene from the story of Joseph – painted when I was seven

Ardwyn Grammar School

My parents must have realised that the quality of teaching in Mynach Primary school left something to be desired, because at the age of nine (as I sat my 11-plus at the age of ten) I was sent to the vicarage to receive coaching from the curate. (The Rev. Ifor Williams). This involved going over old 11-plus papers which meant learning the definition of some long little used words. My encounter with yet more arithmetic brought no success and the Rev Williams called me 'Mary Careless Lewis'. When I eventually sat the 11-plus and wrote all my answers on the question paper so that my father could check, it was discovered that all my answers were wrong. By some miracle I passed in spite of this and in due course, beginning in September 1945, caught the 8 o'clock Crosville Bus to travel the twelve miles to Aberystwyth to attend Ardwyn Grammar School.

As soon as I arrived in the grammar school I realised that Welsh had a low status compared with English. The common language of the school was English and all the administrative business was conducted in English. But the existence of a Welsh culture and language was acknowledged, and the standard of the teaching of Welsh was high. I benefited from the enthusiastic teaching of W. Beynon Davies, particularly in the sixth form when we were introduced to the great poets of past centuries and had to learn, for example, to be able to identify the different forms of *cynghanedd* and the strict meters. Learning more about the bardic tradition has given me increasing pleasure over the years.

Devil's Bridge was served by a minimal bus service designed for those with jobs in offices or shops in Aberystwyth. So the workers' bus left at 8 am and the return bus left Aberystwyth at 5.30. So at the age of eleven, I left home at 8 am, and for an hour and a half at the end of the school day, those of us travelling on the Devil's Bridge service had to wander the streets in the cold and the wet, surviving sometimes on a bag of crisps. Much of this time was spent in Woolworths, the only warm place, gazing at the counters of knick-knacks. After arriving home at 6.30 pm homework had to be tackled after a much-needed hot meal. After two years of this a special bus was organised for the outlying areas of Devil's Bridge and Ponterwyd, which waited for us outside the school gate.

Ardwyn functioned as a powerhouse of energy, punctuating the school year with rituals and processions. The threatening proximity of 'Doc', the senior mistress, sparked the hasty ramming on of a crumpled velour hat. Prize day and the annual Eisteddfod required the formation of a 'crocodile' from the school on the hill to the King's Hall (the Hall was demolished, sadly, in 1989); white shirts to be worn over cardigans and under gym slips to ensure a uniform pattern of black and white when the body of pupils was viewed en masse from the balconies of the King's Hall.

On first entering the awesome establishment, the grammar school, the little girl from Pontarfynach was amazed to see all staff members dressed in black gowns which gave them a foreign and somewhat threatening air. Some of the gowns were threadbare and moth-eaten, no longer black but transformed over years of into a mouldy grey-green. The gown for some teachers served as a dramatic teaching aid, swirled and wrapped, rather like a modern dance combined with dramatic voice and gesture calling all to attention.

The school year was divided into time-consuming extra-curricular activities. Autumn term was dominated by a production of a Gilbert and Sullivan opera, expertly produced by the PE teacher. Many of the pupils were talented singers and Ardwyn began the careers of many actors and writers. My daughter Sianed is a professional musician, but I had no confidence to join these productions and lack of suitable transport made joining after-school activities impossible, but the art department was encouraged to produce posters for the productions and I more than once received a prize for a poster design.

The spring term was dominated by the inter-house Eisteddfod, held on 1 March, St David's Day. Every break time was devoted to choir practice and everyone was encouraged to take part either as a performer for solos and recitations or writing stories essays or poems, in English and in Welsh. I once won a prize for a short story.

All sports were considered to be of the utmost importance and included an annual sports day, cross-country running, rugby, hockey, netball, tennis, cricket and gymnastics. Every year there was a mock election with candidates for Plaid Cymru, and the Liberal, Labour and Conservative parties. These elections generated much passion and excitement, with party speakers giving presentations at breaktimes and in the lunch hour. Debating was developed to a high standard. Two of my contemporaries cut their teeth on debates in Ardwyn, and went on to Westminster: John Morris (now Lord Morris of Blaenafon), Secretary of State for Wales from 1974 to 1979, and Elystan Morgan (now Lord Elystan Morgan), Labour member for Ceredigion between 1966 and 1974.

Social life was limited during my time in Ardwyn. Children who were bussed in from the villages were always a little apart from those who lived in town. The bus service to Pontarfynach did not allow one to join in after-school activities, and weekends were equally difficult. Aberystwyth children, with some exceptions, were more likely to be non-

Welsh-speaking, so the comparatively low status of Welsh created a difference between those from the country and those from the town. In recent years I have been surprised to discover that some of my contemporaries, whom I took to be monoglot English-speaking townies, could in fact speak Welsh. This, of course, is an unexceptional example of what happens when one language has a higher status than another. And it is, of course, how languages are lost.

Like all grammar schools in Wales, Ardwyn was modelled on English public schools. The school was divided into houses and a competitive spirit was encouraged. Amongst the pupils, the stars undoubtedly were those who excelled at sport; their status was even higher than those who excelled academically. Being very poor and indeed not interested in any sport my salvation in the status stakes was the fact that I seemed to be 'good at art'. As a survival tactic, therefore, I worked hard at this marginal subject. As a result I improved my skill and found that this activity was rewarding and pleasurable. Escaping from the grief of appalling performance at sport inadvertently made me increasingly dependent on the relief I found in drawing and painting.

It was during my time at Ardwyn that I learnt to move between two unconnected worlds, home and school, which must ever remain apart. Rhiwmynach had no modern conveniences. Water had to be carried from the village pump, lighting came from oil lamps and candles – although my father had constructed an erratic electricity services harnessing power from a stream at the bottom of the garden, which proved to be very unreliable. Under these conditions boiling a kettle on the fire was the only way to get hot water, keeping clean was never easy and lack of privacy made the problem worse. The life of my contemporaries in Aberystwyth – living in houses served by mains electricity with the luxury of bathrooms and flushing toilets – was another world. My aim was to to keep these two worlds apart, so that no one from school could be invited home, as revealing the shame of the *tŷ bach* at the end of the garden was more than I could face. My greatest worry when inviting John (who became my husband) home to meet my family was how he would react to the primitive conditions in Rhiwmynach. To my amazement, he thought everything was wonderful and remembered best my mother's cooking.

I now place a great value on my early years in a thinly-populated rural environment. It was as a teenager that I first encountered the low status accorded to everything connected with the rural, contrasted with the high status given to urban living. Scorn for all things rural is not restricted to Wales but is in fact a global phenomenon. I quote the Scottish poet Iain Crichton Smith:

> [Gaelic] is associated with peasants, with the folk. There is a feeling even among Highlanders who go off to Glasgow or Edinburgh that it marks them in some way as inferior people. The English imperialist thrust has done its work well – contempt for Gaelic is planted deep within the Highland consciousness itself.

> *Anglo-Welsh Review*, spring 1972

It was at this time that I first experienced belonging to the periphery. Surviving the tensions created has no doubt given me the resolve to survive in difficult circumstances.

Penlonfedw family – Mary's mother Beryl between David Lloyd and Sarah Ann

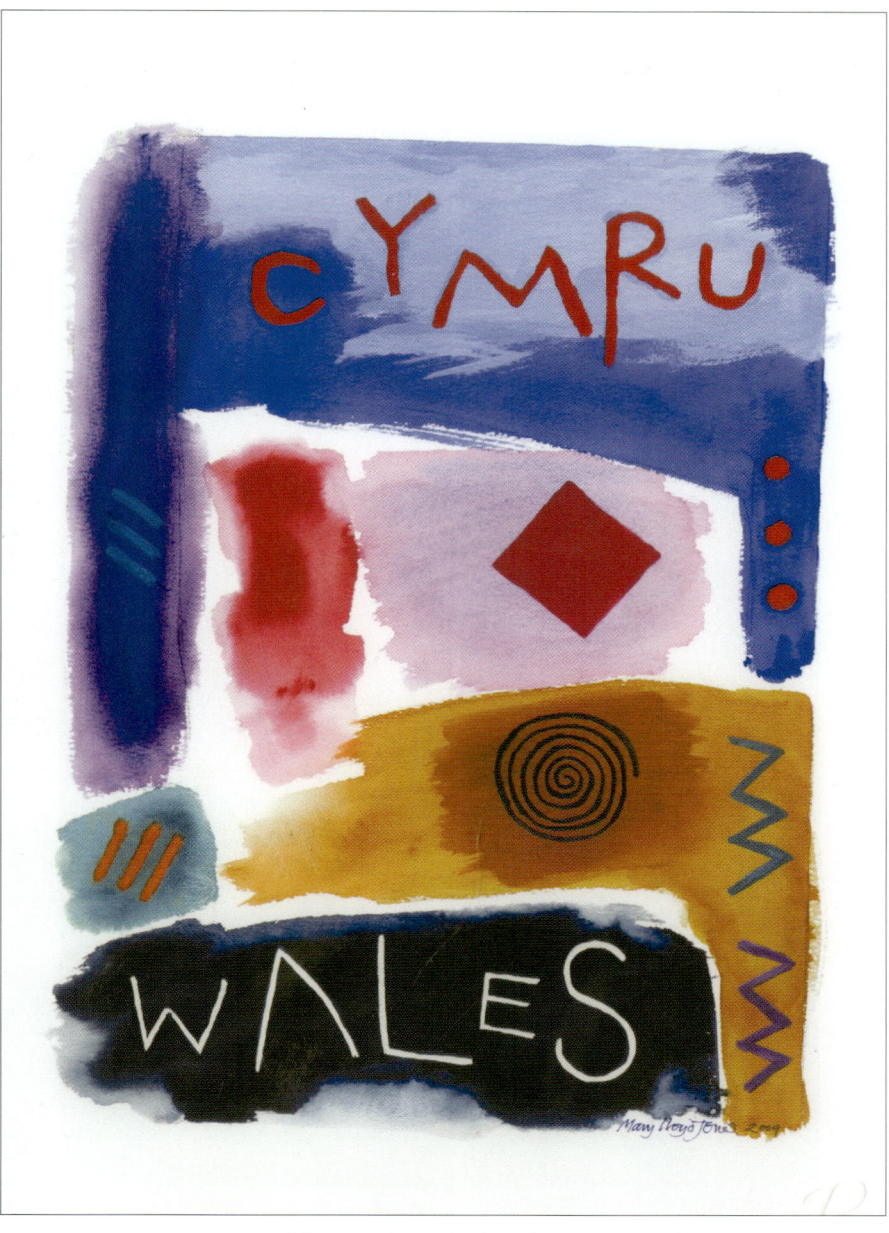

Banner celebrating the Wales/Smithsonian Festival,
Washington DC (2009)

Barclodiad y Gawres, mixed media, 107'5mm x 67mm (2003)

Detail of the quilt made by my great-grandmother Grace Jones

Cwm Rheidol, watercolour 12' x 16" (1984)

Cwm Rheidol, oil on canvas, 3ft x 4ft (1990)

Swyn, mixed media, 107'5mm x 67.5mm

Cliff, Aberarth, mixed media 10' x 14" (1961/2)

Frongoch Mine, mixed media 22' x 30' (2014)

Bryn Celli Ddu, mixed media 12" x 16" (2003)

The Colour of Saying: Exhibition at Aberystwyth Arts Centre (2001)

Banners hanging outside the National Museum Wales, for the duration of the Cardiff National Eisteddfod (2008)

Penlonfedw

My mother was the eldest of ten children born to Sarah Ann and David Lloyd, grocer and butcher, of Penlonfedw, a smallholding supporting three cows, a pig, chickens, and a horse that drew a trap, which travelled to neighbouring villages delivering fresh meat and groceries once a week. My grandmother had a trotting gait, a half-run, as completing all the tasks necessary for survival could only be achieved by travelling in the fast lane. My grandfather, David Lloyd a silent man, spent his time seated, smoking a pipe, and only exerted himself when loading the trap, or later the car, for his weekly rounds. My grandmother did the milking; my grandfather sitting on a wooden crate looked on whilst smoking his pipe. Three of my mother's sisters married and moved to live in Carmarthen, London and Ton Pentre, whilst the youngest, Auntie Megan, stayed at home, helped with running the shop and cared for her parents in their old age. It was an accepted custom that the youngest daughter remained at home providing a multi-dimensional care service that was there to support, as needed, all three generations of the Lloyd family. My mother was the only one of Sarah Ann and David's married daughters who remained at home, in Devil's Bridge.

Every summer saw an invasion of cousins, who provided me with much appreciated companionship. The need to visit the family home once a year shaped the pattern of time, and the summer holidays brought a joyful reunion for all the cousins. The days were organised so that certain walks were accomplished every year. The aunts and uncles took us to visit Parson's Bridge, where we bounced on rickety planks strung across the swirling waters of the river Rheidol. Another walk was around Trisant or to visit an old mill on the way to Llaneithr. These walks sometimes included a picnic or an organised gathering of whinberries. Repeated walking over the same terrain over many years has no doubt embedded a connection with these places that is now a store of images that emerge in my paintings. My parents could never find the time or the energy to take part in these walks. My aunts all lived in houses that had bathrooms, electricity, and modern conveniences, and had succeeded in acquiring material comforts that my parents did not possess. I was aware of these differences, but at the time enjoying the companionship of the cousins banished any negative thoughts.

Devil's Bridge was not attached to mains electricity until 1953 and during my time in school water had to be carried from the village pump 100 yards away. Drinking water from a spring for Penlonfedw had to be carried for a quarter of a mile. My father had fixed up an electricity generating system using water captured from a stream in the garden to run a generator. This system served a few low-powered light bulbs – erratically. A local farmer (who lived at Tynrhyd) harnessed the power from a fast-flowing stream that dropped many hundreds of yards into the Rheidol river. This system even powered one street light, as well as serving all the houses clustered around the post office and the war memorial. However, every autumn falling leaves clogged the pipes and all the men had to assist in sorting out the problem so that the lights could be switched on again. In summer lack of sufficient water would be a problem. I recall my mother telephoning 'Willy Tynrhyd' to ask if he could turn on the generator so that she could do some ironing.

Today much controversy exists over the development of wind farms. Many households in Devil's Bridge during the 1940s and 50s installed solitary windmills which could provide modest lighting for a few rooms. Wind power was the choice of those who were not within reach of water-powered electricity.

The contrast between these conditions and today's comforts of central heating and plentiful light is startling. We had a fire in only one room, my mother supplemented cooking facilities by also using a paraffin stove. Tilley lamps provided reasonable light, but that was for the living room only. Candles were used in the bedrooms and my determination to spend many hours reading by candlelight was probably responsible for my need for spectacles when I was in my mid teens.

Today electronic entertainment from a myriad of digital technological gadgets, multiplying seemingly weekly at a bewildering rate, assaults one's consciousness and, unless controlled, leaves no space for quiet reflection.

In the 1930s and 40s the wireless brought the outside world of music hall, dramas, politics and most importantly news into Rhiwmynach. Listening to the news required everyone to cease talking. Another programme that demanded complete silence was Tommy Handley's *ITMA*, which left all doubled up in laughter. *Noson Lawen* with 'Triawd y Coleg' from Bangor on Radio Cymru was a great favourite and not to be missed. For me, *Awr y Plant* (children's hour); *Galw Gari Tryfan*, a hugely successful detective series, required complete silence from all the family so that I should miss no important clues.

I believe my father inherited the ancient art of the storyteller. The aunts and uncles and cousins visiting in their turns always demanded some stories. On winter nights neighbours and friends would gather to listen to his endless repertoire of tales from the recent past, of minor catastrophies, comic characters and amusing incidents. Some of these stories dealt with darker material, tales of corpse-candles associated with particular places and of the astonishing skills of the '*cwnjer*' (conjurer) who could undo spells and curses and cure burns at great distances. Through these stories I glimpsed an older world that was mysterious and irrational. These tales cemented a permanent relationship and sense of belonging to the village and its environs for all who heard them. My father was a skilled performance artist. Each presentation was delivered with pauses designed to create suspense. The timing was leisurely, demanding complete focus and attention. The audience was usually familiar with the material, waiting with bated breath for the punchline – which, unfortunately, was frequently lost as my father collapsed into a helpless attack of laughter. The stories were punctuated by audience laughter, and my father joining in.

My brother David sleeping (1949)

A Sunday School Trip

Today it is considered normal and expected that everyone has at least one annual holiday, an opportunity to travel to foreign countries and to experience other cultures. I can recall none of our neighbours in Devil's Bridge in the 1930s and 40s or even 50s ever going on holiday. My parents never had a vacation, the responsibilities of caring for the animals and my invalid Uncle Phillip, and, of course, lack of money made the concept an impossibility. After the end of the war, in 1945, a Sunday School trip became once more a possibility with the easing of petrol restrictions. This was the only way that experience of the world outside the the 2 or 3 square miles was possible. For many years both adults and children had attended Welsh-language chapel Sunday Schools. Although the Sunday School at Mynach Chapel did not have a large adult attendance, and my brother and I were the only children, a thirty-seater bus was filled without difficulty, and we experienced our first Sunday School trip, a journey to Pwllheli in Gwynedd. The dramatic landscape of Snowdonia experienced on this journey filled me with amazement. The enormous boulders scattered on the precipitous slopes and the great height of the mountains were in total contrast to the boggy expanses of Ceredigion.

The architecture of the houses built from giant boulders was an entirely new experience and kept me glued to the window. It must have been the first time that I realised the huge variety that makes up the landscape of Wales. After experiencing America, India, Africa and Europe, recalling my response to that early journey – that excitement felt resulting from a mainly visual experience – has shaped my decisions to attempt to recreate the situation where this might happen. Although the whole of Wales is a place that I have explored for seven decades, it is the astonishing variety that can be experienced on relatively short journeys, leading to ever-new discoveries, that provide the themes for my work.

*My brother David and me, with a pet lamb
(1952)*

Cardiff College of Art
1951–56

My mother, her sisters, my grandmothers all followed the tradition of being full-time carers, skilled in the domestic arts and providing the labour required alongside the men in running a smallholding. Women stayed at home and none had shown any desire to be any kind of artist or to have a career. The step that I managed to take in becoming an art student in 1951 is all the more startling as I had no role model. The Beveridge Report, published in 1942, which led to the establishment of the Welfare State in 1948, created now almost unimaginable opportunities for education which had been denied to my parents' generation and all who came before. I recall my father making a special journey to talk to my headmaster to confirm that I would be entitled to a full grant if accepted for a place in an art college.

Very few pupils went to art school from Ardwyn. I was eager to leave home to discover the big world outside – so I rejected the Art Department at Aberystwyth University in favour of Cardiff. An aunt who lived in London had heard of the Slade School, but instinct told me that handling the contrast between Devil's Bridge and London might be too much. I was just seventeen and had completed A-levels. Everyone in Ardwyn was on a fast track.

I realise that today despite the fact that students from Wales receive better support than those in England, with the prospect of student loans and high fees any kind of tertiary education for anyone in my circumstances would be impossible. My entry into art school was dependent on the full grant, for on this I could survive for a term – leaving one pound for the fare home on the Western Welsh bus. Fees were paid by Ceredigion local authority.

Anyone going to art school from Ardwyn was such a rare

event that my art teacher mistook the date for entry application forms. The result was that I was given a late interview days before the beginning of term with no time to find accommodation. I therefore – as a temporary measure – went to stay with my aunt in Ton Pentre, travelling by train daily to Cardiff. The 'temporary measure' lasted for one year.

When I began travelling on the train, I discovered that a group of fellow art students made this daily journey from the towns of the Rhondda Fawr valley, from Ystrad, Dinas, Pentre and Tonypandy. I was shocked on my first day to see the slag heaps and black dereliction visible from the train. The contrast with the green empty spaces of Ceredigion could not be greater. But I quickly realised that my fellow students saw nothing remarkable from the windows, so I never shared my strong reactions. I always endeavoured to hide the fact that I came from a different place.

The quality of the course I found in Cardiff College of Art was a considerable disappointment. Compared with the challenges of A-levels at Ardwyn the syllabus of the Intermediate course in Art and Design seemed infantile and poorly structured when viewed in later years, and worst of all lacking any training in the history of art. Thomas Jones Pencerrig, a brilliant artist from Wales 200 years before his time, only came to my awareness several decades after my time in Cardiff College of Art.

My daily journey on the train, however, more than made up for these defects. This journey proved to be the moving Art Academy; older students (ex-servicemen) like Ernie Zobole, Gwyn Evans, David Mainwaring and Nigel Flowers led discussions about Gauguin, Mattisse and Bonnard. Painting was a serious business and involved constant effort and hard work, this is what I learnt. My sketch book was inspected daily, all my fellow travellers had sketch books which were in constant use. Comments were made and efforts compared. It was at this time that I learnt the focused direction that was needed to produce worthwhile work.

The majority of students at Cardiff Art College travelled daily from the valleys, or were native to Cardiff. During the whole of my five years as a student I encountered only one or two who were Welsh-speaking. Coming from rural Ceredigion I was certainly something of an oddity and I quickly decided to be as like my peers as possible. My first language was buried – but not forgotten – and following the pattern set in school I kept home and college quite separate.

Drawing and painting came relatively easily for me. Nevertheless, I had to plead with the principal for a whole term before he allowed me to study Painting Special, as opposed to Painting Main with embroidery subsidiary in my third year, for the National Diploma in Design. He tried to persuade me that embroidery would be more useful if I wanted a post teaching at art college level. The implication here of course was that painting was a male domain and that

The Arts Ball Cabaret 1953 – I am standing in the centre

women would have limited opportunities (at all levels, no doubt). By the time I left Cardiff at the end of five years the glass ceiling on ambition was firmly in place. We were told that Cardiff Art School students became first-class teachers. There was no mention of their becoming first-class artists. A rare event was a student gaining a place at the Royal College in London. Charles Burton, a Rhondda boy, was one, and his name was mentioned with awe. In 1956 female students were not expected to be ambitious and no tutor ever suggested that I might apply for a place. The lack of confidence generated by this institution, together with my need not to stand out from the crowd in any way, meant that thoughts of the advantage of a period at the Royal College or the Slade did not cross my mind until many years later. I realised how useful in the survival as an artist stakes those letters ARCA would have been.

Elizabeth Jones, a distant relative

Finding a Voice

Although I spent five years at art college, apart from those dynamic tutorials on the train I consider myself to be self taught. The syllabus followed to get the NDD (National Diploma in Design) in painting meant painting figuratively in the subdued impressionist style of the group known as the Euston Road group. The foundation of this method was based on life drawing supported with preparatory charcoal studies before painting in oils. Whilst this grounding was useful, its limitations were frustrating. I was hungry to understand Mattisse and Gauguin's use of colour and the rationale behind cubism, surrealism and all the other isms that developed in the early years of the twentieth century. To make up for these defects I was determined to visit as many exhibitions as possible. I believe that I visited most important Exhibitions in London from 1958 to 1998 in an effort to harvest as many ideas as possible in order to decide on my own path forward. I learnt much basic art history as an extra-mural tutor for Aberystwyth University from about 1975 to 1985 when I taught art history in Llandrindod Wells, Aberbanc and Haverfordwest. Teaching a subject is, of course, the best way to learn it.

Painting in the manner of the Euston Road group our subjects on the NDD painting course were compositions based on urban streets and buildings incorporating a minimum of three figures. Many years later I realised how alien these subjects were for me. Whilst I managed to create acceptable compositions in the required manner, it was only when I started painting again in Aberarth in 1961 that I began to recognise the source material to which I could respond with enthusiasm. No one in Cardiff suggested that

I should create compositions using material from my own rural background.

The particular conjunction of natural and man-made forms that I found in Aberarth seemed to suggest endless compositions and possibilities. As I walked through the village, taking the girls to school or taking an evening stroll, paintings appeared around every corner. Colour has always been my passion and my task was to achieve the courage to orchestrate colour freely whilst rooting composition in elements lifted from the seen world. Abstraction held the most attractive possibilities, but I instinctively felt the need to be grounded in the lived experience of place. I was struggling to understand which was the best way forward when I hit on a direction that combined several viewpoints in one composition. In this way I killed the domination of Renaissance perspective. I found a new freedom by looking in one direction, making some marks on my sheet of paper, then turning to look in opposite direction. Sometimes I turned the paper upside down. In this way I found that I could create new shapes, which could be flat or textured, but still related to my experience of place. I worked in this way for three or four years from 1961–1965.

Knowledge that has come to me long after the period in Cardiff emphasises the missed opportunities that could have made life a lot easier. Heinz Koppel was a Jewish refugee from Berlin who had been living with his parents in Prague, but he and his father had fled to Britain. Heinz' mother was killed in the Treblinka concentration camp. Heinz lived in Dowlais and worked in Merthyr Tydfil during my period in college. Ernie Zobole visited him and was evidently an important influence on his development and created a direct link with ideas circulating on the continent before the war. Heinz and his family lived in London and Liverpool for a while, and his work became well-known;

later he came to live near Aberystwyth, in Cwmerfyn. He died in 1980, aged 61. Sadly, Heinz Koppel was never invited to speak to students in Cardiff, which was a great loss to my generation.

Life during the 1960s in Aberarth and from 1966 in Aberaeron was joyful; our girls went to school and I was sustained by a constant drive to paint the hills, bogs, cliffs and seashore of Ceredigion. I was able to exchange ideas and get a response to work in progress from John, who was developing his work as a printmaker, at this time in screen printing and lino printing. We bought our first house in Aberaeron because it had two large basement rooms which we used as studios. There were no other artists with whom we could share our ambitions and opportunities for funded artist's residencies and exhibiting support had yet to be developed. A supportive environment to make art did not exist in west Wales at this time.

Around about 1969 or 70, in order to understand more about colour, I abandoned all reference to my surroundings, the village, the cliff and the sea, and embarked on a series of purely abstract geometric works. I worked on systematic colour sequences on canvases 6 feet x 4 feet and 4 feet x 4 feet. Here I acknowledge the influence of David Tinker, who had taught us at Cardiff College of Art and was now Head of the Visual Art Department in Aberystwyth University. In 1971 I was accepted as the only female member of the 56 Group Wales, a body of professional artists, mainly staff members of Cardiff and Newport College of Art. Membership of this group, showing in France, Italy and Germany as well as in Wales, was a considerable confidence boost for me in an otherwise bleak situation.

Even this year, 2014 debates on the subject of gender inequality appear regularly in the media and the disadvantages suffered by women in all fields of endeavour have not been eliminated. My position as a solitary female for eight years in the 56 Group Wales (after which another female artist joined the membership of twenty or so) was not comfortable, and I frequently felt invisible in group meetings. This, however, only made me more determined to stay and hold my ground.

To have a career as a painter whilst living in west Wales seemed at times to be an impossible dream. A popular interest in craft, however, developed following the V&A exhibition 'The Craftsman's Art'. Feeling the need to develop an audience for the visual arts in Ceredigion, perhaps we thought visual art could be made accessible to more people through the practice of a craft.

After seeing an exhibition of Polish weaving at the Edinburgh Festival, I became convinced that I should move into the textile fields of weaving and dyeing as this held more hope of a positive response compared with painting. It was at this point that I proceeded down the wrong turning and wasted several years and much energy barking up the wrong tree. This I can appreciate in retrospect, and it is only after returning to the joy of painting that I realised my mistake.

The multitude of ideas for themes and directions which reached me through art magazines and visits to exhibitions, mainly in London, whilst exciting and stimulating, made it difficult to decide which direction to take in my own work. Reading what other artists have written on this problem helped. Barbara Hepworth said: 'Perhaps what one wants to say is formed in childhood and the rest of one's life is spent trying to say it'.

Making Art is a process of self-discovery. Reflecting on this problem and putting my trust in intuition, I concluded that the rural environment of Ceredigion had to be my starting point. It is being outside, walking in a big empty countryside, experiencing the weather, the light and the seasons that always gives me the 'wow' reaction that can give me the boost of energy to begin a painting. I do not believe that I would be a painter if I had to live in a city.

Sianed and me in Romford, Essex

Me with Gudrun

Climate Change

The move from Romford in Essex to Aberaeron in Ceredigion in 1961 provided the first opportunity to get involved in painting five years after leaving college. For the first time after school days I could reconnect with the environment that could provide me with the stimulus and drive to paint.

My daughters were by this time two and four but I found it possible to juggle housework and childcare with spurts of work in the studio, which occupied the best room in our rented cottage by the sea in Aberarth. The stimulus of being by the sea, the cliffs, lanes, gardens and organic character of the huddled houses and rooftops resulted in plenty of energy and ambition to produce new work.

With hindsight, ambitions to function as a serious artist from a base in west Wales must be doomed to failure. The received wisdom was that good art is produced only in London or New York. Artists need an audience and to be part of a supportive community.

The only gallery in west Wales at this time was in the National Library in Aberystwyth. Modern art, especially abstraction, was incomprehensible to most of the population, and it is no exaggeration to state that visual art was regarded with some hostility in comparison with music and literature.

The decision to stay in west Wales resulted in the idea of attempting to change the climate for the visual arts through whatever means presented themselves. The first project in this direction was the establishment of the Aberaeron Art Society in 1962. This organisation celebrated its fiftieth anniversary in 2012. John, potter Geraint Evans and I set up the organisation and negotiated the use of an empty shop owned by Ceredigion County Council on a prominent corner site in the centre of Aberaeron to be used as a gallery for a limited period. George Chapman, an established artist with a London gallery, who achieved fame painting the Rhondda Valleys, lived in Aberaeron with his wife Kate, also an artist, and agreed to exhibit. The other exhibitors were mainly members of the painting evening class I taught in the winter months. Newcomers, some with cottages in the area, were welcomed as exhibitors, as was established illustrator, jeweller and designer, Margaret Holgate.

The London House exhibitions succeeded in raising the profile of the artists and was a focal point of interest in the town during the summer months. Hanging the exhibition and the opening was an excuse for a party, as was the dismantling of the show. The first work that I ever sold was from the Aberaeron Exhibition.

Felinfach Summer School

A brand new Theatre and Arts Centre was opened in Felinfach, Ceredigion, to a fanfare of publicity and celebration in 1972. Inspecting the brochures and posters revealed that no provision had been made for visual art. Impulsively I telephoned the director of Further Education and asked why the visual arts were not mentioned in the programme for the opening of the arts centre.

'Why, you are quite right, *fy merch fach i* [my dear girl]' he said. 'Let us have some ideas.'

John and I immediately set to work organising a week of visual arts activities to be held in the Felinfach Agricultural College, which we called the Aeron Summer School, modelled, we hoped, on the famous Barry Summer School. The summer school opened in July 1973 and was funded by Cardiganshire Education Authority, West Wales Association for the Arts and The Extra Mural Department of the University College of Wales, Aberystwyth. The following courses were on offer for the first year: Experimental Textiles, Colour and Construction, Landscape Painting, Etching and Screen Printing.

John and I negotiated all the funding, and the transformation of the rooms used for agricultural studies so that they could be used for visual arts practice. John also arranged all the bed and breakfast accommodation by telephone for around forty or fifty students. In addition, a series of evening events, including concrete poetry with Bob Cobbing, light shows and puppet performances were organised from our house in Aberaeron. Arthur Giardelli gave an Art History lecture. Our enthusiasm and youth gave us the energy to achieve what was a mammoth task of organisation.

After three successful years, our funding was cut so the experiment was short-lived and the two-man organisation was not sustainable. However, the success of the venture gave us the confidence to embark on running our own Summer School.

Yr Hen Ysgol, Aberbanc

John and I had nourished a dream of acquiring a suitable building which we could transform into a focus for the visual arts thereby passing on our enthusiasm for creativity into the communities surrounding us in west Wales. Our hope was that this project over which we had complete control would counterbalance those feelings of exclusion and marginalisation created by the seeming hopelessness of ever exhibiting work in London. At this time in the early seventies the structures did not exist in Wales that could give the visual arts a platform. The support for artists in the form of funded residencies and assistance with exhibiting costs were to develop only in the following decades. In 1975 when we embarked on our adventure in Yr Hen Ysgol the audience for visual arts in West Wales did not exist so we set about creating one.

During the seventies I was teaching two or three days per week on the foundation course in what was then Dyfed College of Art. Seeing an old school advertised in *Exchange and Mart* I called to visit it in Aberbanc on my way home from Carmarthen to Aberaeron. It turned out to be an architectural gem built in stone and slate, a school with three spacious classrooms attached to a headmaster's house and a large tarmac yard in the centre of the hamlet of Aberbanc. It had been unused as a school for five years, Ceredigion Authority having built a new school across the road (which as a piece of architecture was in every way inferior to the original Victorian school). The building, which we were able to buy, needed repairs to the roof and windows but we could claim the £1600 grant towards installing a bathroom in the house and connecting to the mains drainage.

We moved in in a snowstorm in January 1976 and embarked on running a Summer School the following summer. Following the success of the Craftsman's Art Exhibition at the V&A we felt we felt that concentrating on craft techniques was the best way to engage those who might lack the confidence to draw and paint to take the first step into a creative experiment was through craft.

For this reason we decided to offer prospective students tuition in weaving and spinning, batik and print making, in addition to drawing and painting. John had inherited a collection of looms and spinning wheels after the retirement of a colleague in Aberaeron Comprehensive School and had attended a weaving course at Bradford College so these newly acquired skills broadened the scope of what could be offered at Yr Hen Ysgol. Over a period of ten years we successfully ran our Summer School, made many lifelong friends and welcomed students from France, Germany, Switzerland, USA, Scandinavia, Australia and Japan, in addition to a large number from other parts of Britain and, of course, Wales. Doing this required plenty of energy and careful planning.

Me in my studio in Aberbanc

I continued to teach two or three days per week and John continued as full-time head of the Art department at Aberaeron Comprehensive school. Every April or May I began to fill the freezer with soups for student lunches and wholesome cakes for tea in readiness for the arrival of students in July. Combining teaching with catering and serving meals was certainly demanding but at the time, although often exhausting, it was enjoyable and stimulating. Unfortunately I never felt that we were increasing our income in a truly dramatic way but merely providing the finances necessary to maintain the building.

In addition to attracting students from elsewhere, we were determined to make connections with local communities. This happened in two ways. The Extra-mural Department of Aberystwyth University were happy for me to run a History of Art class combined with life drawing at Yr Hen Ysgol during the winter months. The programme for the evening consisted of two hours of drawing, followed by an hour of art history illustrated with slides. This class proved to be very popular, with approximately twenty members occupying two classrooms/studios, and ran from 1977–1985. The West Wales Arts Association was at this time running a scheme called 'Artists on Tour'. I offered to join this scheme if community groups could visit my studio instead of my travelling to them.

Requests to visit my studio came mainly from *Merched y Wawr* (daughters of the dawn). These were Welsh-language versions of Women's Institute groups; one group was established in all the villages of Welsh-speaking west Wales. Many members of these groups lived on farms and very few would have any interest in the visual arts. I therefore decided to collect examples of historic domestic textiles primarily so that I could discuss the quality of the design and colour generally and make a connection with objects that were familiar to them. For this purpose I began to collect examples of weaving, *carthenni* and blankets like those produced in my grandfathers *'ffatri'*, patchwork quilts and rag mats. I did not mention painting as I felt that this might be for them a foreign and alienating subject. The high spot of the evening was when I demonstrated how to spin on the spinning wheel and on one memorable occasion twenty women together began to sing a spinning song. I should confess also that every so often one or two would fall asleep. These were farming women who spent all day on hard physical work in the fresh air.

Quilt Masterpiece
One of my most treasured possessions is a 'log cabin' quilt made by Grace, my great-grandmother, and given to me by my father's sister Dilys when I was in my early forties. This is an accomplished piece of art, a traditional geometric design made from strips of cloth 1 cm wide. It demonstrates a skill in measurement, calculation and fine sewing, with the assembling of hundreds of tiny pieces of cloth to create a unified design. Here I see an intelligent understanding of colour relationships and tonal values. These are all attributes that are needed when I orchestrate colour in my painting.

Making the connection between the mathematical skills of my great-great-grandfather, shipbuilder Dafydd Jones, and the splendour of his daughter's stitched artwork has happened only as I write. David Jones, in *Epoch and Artist*, wrote:

> The bards of an earlier Wales referred to themselves as 'carpenters of song'. Carpentry suggests a fitting together, as you know; the English word 'artist' means, at root, someone concerned with a fitting of some sort.

My studio in Aberbanc

The master ship-builder and his daughter were both practising what can be described as 'carpentry'.

New Possibilities
In addition to attempting to increase the support and understanding of the visual arts a large proportion of time and energy was spent on teaching. The main reason for buying Yr Hen Ysgol was to provide ideal studio space with light and high ceilings that could be utilised to make ambitious work. So, I was able to explore new ideas and media using the luxury of a big studio after moving to Aberbanc.

The experiment of running a summer school and winter art classes continued while we were also accommodating the friends and fellow students of our daughters: Gudrun, a textile student at the Surrey College of Art and Design in Farnham, and Sianed, a music student in Dartington College of the Arts, Devon. The young people flowed in and out, making music, making felt, weaving, and at one point running a theatre company called '33 1/3'. One young couple arrived to spend their honeymoon with us! Against this backdrop of intense activity my work proceeded; I was exhibiting regularly and taking full advantage of the generous studio space and the acre or so of tarmac.

Accident and coincidence has often influenced new directions taken in the work. The decision to make craft techniques the doorway to tempt hopeful artists into a creative adventure led me to teach myself the technique of using hot wax on cloth known as batik. Pleasing results are possible using batik, even for complete beginners. Following the activity in the Felinfach Summer School, the batik dyes were included in the move to Aberbanc. It was that at this time I discovered that by adding a seaweed-based thickener it was possible to paint with dyes. The results were similar to that of watercolour with a similar luminosity but with the potential for large-scale works. I was able to explore the possibilities of creating irregularly-shaped compositions using themes taken from the landscape, but with the possibility of connecting with the Welsh quilt-making tradition. It was at this time that I began to forge my own visual language in a fluid and flexible technique that opened up possibilities for the layering of references and moving away from received conventions of landscape painting. It is significant that these exciting developments were made possible after the physical upheaval of moving into a new and inspiring work space.

Working conditions as a part-time lecturer in Dyfed College of Art had many shortcomings. No contract was ever issued and each September one was left waiting for the phone call to be told how many hours had been allotted for my contribution. I continued to work under these conditions as it left me with two days in which to continue with my own explorations in the Studio. This pattern continued for fifteen years.

No one was more astonished than I when I was appointed Visual Arts Development Officer for Dyfed – the largest county in square miles in Britain at this time, 1985. One of the tasks advertised in the job description of the Visual Arts Development Officer was to explore the possibility of converting the old School of Art in Carmarthen into a gallery and arts centre. This task naturally had great attraction for me, and from the very first day I set about discovering how this might be achieved. I was fortunate that historian Malcolm Jones was the Mayor of Carmarthen at this time, and he gave me much support and advice including the setting up of The Friends of the Old School of Art. There followed a campaign of publicity including the re-enacting in Victorian costume of the original opening parade in 1892 of the original School of Art. As Visual Arts Development Officer, a post part-funded by the Arts Council of Wales and the Local Authority, I was part of the Cultural Services Department responsible for the Library and Museums Service.

For the next three years I endeavoured to arrange exhibitions in numerous libraries across Dyfed. Making exhibitions was a satisfying creative exercise but I depended on John for help with hanging work and serving the wine in the private views, as no technical assistance had been considered necessary when my post was created. A few libraries had spaces which could serve as galleries, Carmarthen Library being one of these. I managed to transform the large basement room with an exhibition of borrowed quilts, and this I believe was the first ever exhibition of Welsh quilts. These magnificent works of art continue to be undervalued. One of the most exciting developments since 2009 has been the opening of the Welsh Quilt Centre in the Old Court House in Lampeter, showing the extensive collection of the owner Jen Jones in a

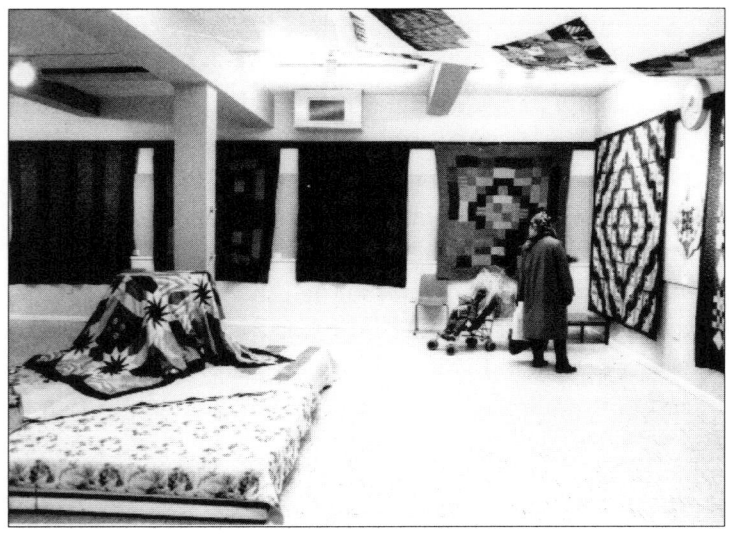

Quilt Exhibition in Carmarthen Library (1986)

succession of themed exhibitions. The importance of the contribution to Welsh visual culture by Jen Jones in preserving and conserving these still undervalued works is a story that still waits to be told.

In my role as Arts Officer my services were requested to make a visual contribution to the Fishguard Music Festival. A link with visual culture in Ireland seemed a good idea as Fishguard had daily ferries to Rosslare. An exhibition of work by Irish artists was organised in due course and for the opening ceremony Bernard Loughlin, director of the Tyrone Guthrie centre was invited to be guest speaker. In his speech Bernard described the setting up and running of the Tyrone Guthrie Centre as a special place where artists in all media could spend time on creative projects whilst being fed and watered in what was the Tyrone Guthrie family home in County Monaghan, north of Dublin. Annaghmacerrig is a typical large country house in a Victorian style of architecture set in acres of countryside.

Bernard extended an invitation to any artists from Wales who might like to have a residency to send a letter of application for a place. Bernard Loughling's invitation was, for me, very attractive and in

Preparing for the 'Celebration of Weaving' exhibition

due course I managed to negotiate five weeks away from my responsibilities within Dyfed Cultural Services.

Viewed retrospectively, this step proved to be a landmark in my career as an artist. Meeting Irish artists, poets, film-makers and composers, in addition to international artists from Israel, Canada and the USA, I was impressed by the confidence expressed by everyone compared with the attitudes of my fellow artists in Wales. After five weeks sharing conversations around the large dining table every evening and visits to arts festivals in neighbouring tiny villages, I was told without hesitation that if you were a serious artist, you practiced your art full time. I decided to take steps to put this into practice on returning to west Wales.

I wrote my letter of resignation on my first morning, after reading a letter giving me a rise in salary, and making what was a two-year appointment permanent. The director of Cultural Services was puzzled by my change of direction. It was a great satisfaction for me, however, when a few years after my departure the Old School of Art was transformed into a gallery, Oriel Myrddin, and is now a centre of excellence providing exhibitions of the highest quality and supporting an education programme for schools and adults. I embarked on my career as a full-time artist in 1989, which happened to be the year that Martin Tinney opened his first gallery, the West Wharf Gallery in Cardiff. He has shown my work regularly ever since.

The Tyrone Guthrie Centre: a Cultural Centre founded on Greatness

Moving into this supportive community of writers, visual artists, dancers, scriptwriters and film makers has generated sufficient adrenaline and creative energy to ensure many months of future work. No comparable establishment exists in Wales – or indeed, Britain.

Ireland is nearer to Wales than London, yet the barrier of the Irish Sea makes this a far more surprising country to visit than either France or Spain. My conclusion is that we know nothing of Ireland, but that we might benefit from looking more closely at our Celtic neighbours.

The Tyrone Guthrie Centre offers artists ideal conditions in which to concentrate on their work. All residents meet each evening for a splendid meal prepared by Mary Loughlin, who must be Ireland's best cook; otherwise, each artist works alone in a studio or study for the whole long uninterrupted day.

My space was a studio in the main house connected to a bedroom and a bathroom. The quiet was total; working time was sacrosanct, and generally one did not visit other artists in their rooms unless invited. Trips to the large kitchen for coffee and survival rations during the day provided opportunities for social contact. Privacy was respected, but one was never lonely. One of the most worthwhile aspects of the experience was the opportunity for the exchange of ideas with other artists; the contact with

Irish poets and visual artists from Canada for me was particularly valuable. The importance of their response to my work cannot be overestimated.

Annaghmakerrig is set in a wooded estate of 400 acres, so painting sessions were interspersed with long walks along muddy tracks around the lake and through the trees. The small towns within ten or fifteen miles of the centre each in turn ran Arts Festivals during October, so in the evenings there were numerous trips to poetry readings, concerts and plays, ending in long discussions in the pub or in the kitchen at Annaghmakerrig. It was in a convent in the town of Monaghan that we had the opportunity to see Brian Friel's play *Making History*. Events in these festivals, in towns the size of Aberaeron or Llandysul, were without exception well-attended, and sponsored largely by local businesses. This was my first experience of joining a queue to get into a poetry reading, apart from at the National Eisteddfod.

My conclusion after this visit was that a far more supportive climate for the arts exists in Ireland than is the case in Britain. This was reflected in the confidence and buoyant attitude of the artists that I met in Annaghmakerrig. Several factors are responsible for this. In 1988, the year that I stayed in Annaghmakerrig, selected artists in all disciplines could receive a pension of £5000 a year for life from the Irish Government. And I met several individuals who had been honoured in this way. No income tax has to be paid on income derived from the practise of one's art. At Annaghmakerrig, Irish artists paid only what they could afford, the remainder being made up by the Irish Arts Council. Ireland is still a poor country compared with Britain; Irish roads are generally full of potholes, and village shops thinly stocked; nevertheless, the arts are given their due importance.

The contrast of this with the current philistine climate in Britain cannot be avoided.

Ireland is one of the countries most adversely affected by the banking crises of 2008. On a recent visit, I discovered that funding for the *Aosdána* scheme of support for artists continues, and has been ring-fenced against cuts, with a sum valued at 2.5 million Euros.

The *Aosdána* scheme creates a climate that makes a career as a practising artist a possibility for those from a non-privileged background. The contrast between bonuses for bankers and brutal cuts in arts funding and welfare in Britain is stark.

Membership of *Aosdána*, which is by peer nomination and election, is limited to 250 living artists who have produced a distinguished body of work. Members must have been born in Ireland or have been resident there for five years, and must have produced a body of work that is original and creative. The current membership is 246. The three disciplines – music, literature and visual arts – receive support from *Aosdána* and membership is now also open to architects and choreographers.

Whilst our first aim after acquiring the Old School was to build on our experience of running the Felinfach Summer School, we always felt that whilst income should be generated to make possible the maintenance of a large old building. We were also convinced that non-money-making projects would be acceptable if they were of interest to us. It was in this way that many unexpected activities found a platform in Aberbanc.

I recall storytelling sessions with Carol Burne Jones; my extra-mural class provided an audience. We hosted a presentation from the famous Findhorn Community in Scotland, which included tales of giant cabbages and extraordinary spiritual events. The Findhorn evening ended with circle dancing, which was popular with many groups at this time. Next door, in Aberbanc, David and Jean Glaister ran a village shop which also had a zinc shed which they renamed 'The Red Barn'. This was a period when west Wales was settled by large numbers of mainly young people looking for self-sufficiency and an alternative lifestyle. This lifestyle embraced 'doing your own thing', which included creating your own theatre whilst rejecting anything like the passivity of television viewing. In the Red Barn Theatre we saw an astonishing range of productions, adaptations of *Hamlet, Macbeth* and Tennessee Williams, as well as original plays written by cast members.

Members of this theatre company came from north Pembrokeshire, the Cardigan area and the Teifi valley. In some ways being a member of the Red Barn audience echoed my childhood memories of plays performed in The Bungalow in Devil's Bridge. Some of the Red Barn troupe

John and me in Aberbanc

were trained actors whilst the rest were talented amateurs. Set design was minimal; sometimes one sat on a sack of coal if all the chairs were occupied. With close proximity to the actors in a tiny space (25 feet square), this was truly theatre in the round, which over time developed its own conventions.

Aberbanc is in a Welsh-speaking stronghold. The Red Barn troupe were exclusively newcomers with no knowledge or interest in the Welsh language. John and I were the only Welsh-speakers ever to join this audience.

Cliff McLucas

One of the most talented individuals to become part of our lives in Aberbanc was Cliff McLucas, who tragically died in 2002. We first knew Cliff in 1976 when he joined my extra-mural class with Karen, his partner. We discovered that he was a joiner and also trained as an architect. He mended a staircase in the old house and when we discovered his extraordinary skills he created a balcony and staircase in one of the large studios, an extraordinary handsome door inspired by Mondrian into the main studio, and later a spiral staircase leading to two study bedrooms in our large sitting room (previously a classroom). Cliff and Karen and their three children were part of the influx of newcomers looking for a self-sufficient life. They kept a cow; Karen made butter and ran a productive garden.

Cliff's enthusiasm could not be confined to one art form. It emerged that he had extensive knowledge of cutting-edge avant garde films. He persuaded us to apply for funding from the Welsh Arts Council that would enable us to show a programme of rarely shown Art House films over a sequence of four evenings. We were successful in our application, and the programme of films was shown, the art class providing a core audience. The material was challenging and included films by Andy Warhol and Carolee Schneemann. This resulted in some of the audience making an early exit. John and I appreciated seeing films that were difficult but opened up new possibilities, and the strong reactions produced made the evenings memorable. It subsequently emerged that Cliff had a burning ambition to realise an art form yet to be named.

Every Christmas the art class held a party in our studios. It was at one of these that Cliff brought into being perhaps his first performance theatre. To the accompaniment of a four-note sequence on the piano (echo of Phillip Glass), one performer walked slowly up and then down the spiral staircase whilst another read very slowly, with rhythmical pauses, a wedding announcement from the *Cambrian News*. The audience was left perplexed, speechless or amused; one or two left.

Following his move from Tregroes to Aberystwyth and the brief flowering of the Barn Centre, Cliff was eventually was able to realise the art form that became Site Specific Theatre following his involvement with the theatre company Brith Gof. Cliff eventually became the director of Brith Gof and during his leadership a succession of innovative and memorable theatrical events happened in unexpected locations, which included a disused factory in Cardiff, a remote forest, a farmyard and a chapel. Many of these productions travelled to Europe, and Welsh theatre could claim to be a leading force combining local with global issues through verbal interaction, music and the possibilities of new media. Cliff learnt Welsh and was committed to giving voice to a marginalised culture.

It is satisfying to note that the National Theatre Company of Wales and Theatr Genedlaethol Cymru are now building on the work of Brith Gof and Cliff McLucas in a number of recent much applauded successes, the most spectacular being perhaps *The Passion in Port Talbot*, staring Michael Sheen.

On 3 February 2013 Theatre Genedlaethol Cymru performed *Y Bont*, commemorating the fiftieth anniversary of the direct action protest for Welsh language rights, which took place on Trefechan Bridge, Aberystwyth. The performance incorporated visits to various cafés in the town, where decisions and plans had been made in 1963, and ended in the Arts Centre with film projections.

In many ways it can be argued that following the campaigns for the Welsh language in 1962 and 63, and subsequently, by *Cymdeithas yr Iaith Cymraeg* [the Society for the Welsh Language, which was formed after the Trefechan Bridge protest), the Welsh language is in a stronger position than the other minority languages in western Europe, such as Gaelic, Breton and Cornish, and that within Britain, Wales has a recognisable separate identity. Whilst much has been achieved in film, television, theatre and publishing since the establishment of S4C and the Welsh Assembly, visual artists in Wales have not developed similar confidence as the deficit continues in the provision of suitable institutions that will develop an audience and allow potential talent to flourish.

Colonial attitudes continue to spread their poison, and even in 2014, in some quarters, little has changed since the Editorial that appeared in *The Times* in 1816:

> Wales, it should be remembered, is a small country, unfavourably situated for commercial purposes, with indifferent soil, and inhabited by an unenterprising people ... All progress and civilisation in Wales has come from England ... the sooner all Welsh specialities disappear from the face of the earth, the better.

David Bell, Arts Officer for the Arts Council of Great Britain, maintained that Wales had no visual art – indeed, no visual culture. In his book *The Artist in Wales*, published in 1957 (a year after I left Cardiff Art College), he states: 'At no time since the Norman Conquest has the Welshman had any visual artistic tradition'. At this point we must overlook the misogyny, but this prejudice is blind to the achievement of the remarkable Thomas Jones (Pencerrig), Richard Wilson, the accepted father of British landscape, or Owen Jones, who published his seminal *Grammar of Ornament* in 1856.

'The idea that the Welsh are nonvisual has been and continues to be damaging to the culture' – Peter Lord, in *The Aesthetic of Relevance*. This perceived congenital deficiency has been my arch-enemy through the decades spent endeavouring to banish and kill it for ever.

Following the funding of the National Museum and

National Library in 1907, the Art Department of the National Museum was opened in 1927. According to Peter Lord, the programme for the opening ceremony of the new museum stated that 'The museum must not attempt to be a copy of the British Museum on a small scale, which happens to be in Wales'. Sadly, a succession of Keepers has failed to foster Welsh artists. The policy has been to supplement perceived gaps in the mainstream European art in the Davies sisters' bequest, which led, for example, to the purchase of *The Entrance to the Grand Canal* by Canaletto, and the acquisition of a Poussin in 1989 for £7.2 million, to be shared with the National Gallery.

'The concerns of Wales are also the concerns of the minority cultures of the rest of the world' – Peter Lord again. It is important to value an indigenous visual culture, to support its development and to value minorities and their relevance in today's global community. I see an opportunity with the prospect of a new use for the Old College in Aberystwyth for a clean start, to create a home for the visual culture of Wales in all its diversity and potential for new forms yet to be conceived. With its varied spaces and almost limitless variety, new art forms could grow here that could link the ideas of Ruskin and William Morris with new technology and its potential for cross-fertilisation between established art forms.

The National Library has consistently focused on showing and supporting Welsh visual culture. Mike Tooby, the first curator of Tate St Ives, moved to the National Museum of Wales to become the Director of Learning, Programmes and Development. He was instrumental in arranging for four banners designed by me to hang outside the museum in Cardiff for the duration of the National Eisteddfod when it was held in Cardiff in 2008. He was also responsible for commissioning three pieces of my work for the new exhibition, Origins, in the Archaeology Gallery. Working with the museum staff in the Department of Archaeology was most rewarding, and an experience I would like to repeat. Mike Tooby was not the keeper of art, but one can but hope that other Welsh artists can become involved in similar projects in the future.

A portrait of myself drawn by a child in one of my school workshops

Survival

Leading a busy life as wife and mother, aspiring artist, teacher, administrator of the Summer School and the art class, I was protected from realising how strong and entrenched those forces were that would prevent me from achieving my ambition of making good art.

In the early eighties I came across the Canadian writer Margaret Atwood's book entitled *Survival*. This is not a novel but an extensive analysis of the effect living in a marginalised culture has on the creativity of its population. Margaret Atwood focuses on the problems faced by aspiring writers in Canada living in the shadow of American culture. Her analysis is strongly applicable to visual artists choosing to work in Wales. Reading this book enabled me to look objectively at my own situation and pick my way through the traps and obstacles into a position where I could value my own work and move forward with more confidence:

> There are two factors involved in the production of 'Great Art': the artist and the audience. The artist acts as a vision or tongue, giving shape to patterns in which the audience may then recognise itself for better or for worse, identify itself. Take away the artist and the audience can never achieve self-knowledge. But take away the audience and the artist has part of himself cut off. He is blocked; he is like a man shouting to no one. Without a sense of his audience he can have no ultimate sense of purpose, no feeling that what he produced has any significance. He is a man talking to himself and talking to oneself is usually considered either a result of isolation or a symptom of insanity.
>
> *Margaret Atwood*

Central to an analysis of the positions of artists in Wales (or writers in Canada) is that Wales as a whole is a victim, or an oppressed minority, or exploited. Let us accept that Wales (Canada) is a colony. A partial definition of a 'colony' is that it is a place from which a profit is made, but not by the people there; the major profit from a colony is made in the centre of the empire. If Wales is a collective victim the Basic Victim positions as outlined by Margaret Atwood are relevant. The positions are the same whether you are a victimised country, a victimised minority group, or a victimised individual.

Basic Victim Positions

Position 1: Denial of the fact that you are a victim. Anger is directed at fellow victims

Position 2: Acknowledgement of the fact that you are a victim but explain that it is Fate, the will of God, biology (women) or decreed by history or economics. Not your fault, resigned to longsuffering, anger at fellow victims and oneself.

Position 3: Acknowledgement of the fact that you are a victim but refuse to accept that it is inevitable. Dynamic position. Real cause of oppression identified. Energy put into constructive action. Repudiation of victim role.

Position 4: Being a creative non-victim. The position of those who have never been victims. In position 4 creative activity of all kinds becomes possible. Energy is no longer being suppressed.

Surviving as an Artist

Against this backdrop of functioning within a marginalised culture, as analysed by Margaret Atwood, the only way to proceed was from position 4. Working towards creating an audience for the visual arts placed us firmly in position 4 as creative non victims. Blaming history, economics or biology would place us back in position 2. For members of a country or a culture, shared knowledge of their place – their 'here' – is not a luxury but a necessity. Without that knowledge they will not survive. For an artist living in a marginalised culture, the most damaging concept is that great art is only made by dead foreigners. For a female in the same situation the perception that great art was only produced by male artists deepens the poison. Functioning away from access to the centrist hub of London or New York the work produced will generally be labelled 'second-rate', 'provincial' or 'regional'.

The horns of the dilemma for artists on the margins can be expressed like this:

> Stay in the culture and be crippled as an artist or 'escape into nothing'.
>
> *Margaret Atwood*

From necessity I discovered that domestic tasks could be woven into painting time in the studio. The kitchen was always near to the studio so walking away from a few brush strokes or leaving some water colour to settle and dry gave me that important thinking time whilst I could be occupied preparing vegetables or keeping an eye on the oven. I should point out that no one was ever poisoned as a result of this multi-tasking. Painting is an art of speedy action interspersed with pauses. The time taken for reflection is a crucial part of the process. That this time should be clear of interruption is another essential factor. Becoming an artist is a long process of self-discovery. If conditions are favourable for the necessary length of time a personal language will evolve.

Now in my eighth decade I can identify the basic requirements for creative endeavour. First is the need for 'A room of one's own', in the words of Virginia Woolf. The next basic requirement is support from the nearest family. My ability to continue working has been wholly dependent on the understanding and encouragement I received from John. We worked as a team on all our joint projects. In all this I was fortunate as many aspiring women artists do not have a studio space, and are trapped in the demands of others and are not able to block interruptions.

When a working space and supportive relationships have been achieved there are other requirements if great art or at least good art can be achieved. Time management is

Me in my studio in Aberbanc (1978)

essential so that blocks of studio time clear of other demands will make focused concentration possible. To begin a body of work a minimum of three days is necessary. Silence and solitude must be respected by family, friends and inquisitive neighbours. This is not easily achieved, and requires skills in diplomacy on the part of the artist to avoid misunderstandings, crossed lines and worse.

When I first began painting in Aberarth, five years after leaving college, the dissatisfaction and anger towards the bad work that I produced left me despairing of climbing out of this pit of hopelessness. What kept me going was a stubborn determination. And living in an environment that was a daily inspiration. The land, the gardens, the sea, the cliffs and the bogs compelled me to paint. I began to realise that understanding the rhythms of the creative process would help me to move through the steps involved in making art. I began to explore books on psychology, Jung in particular with his analysis of the subconscious and the importance of archetypes. This material drew me towards the idea of a hidden world that visual images could reveal.

Beginning a painting is possible only if one has the surge of enthusiasm and conviction that this time the composition will be the best ever, a masterpiece no less. Placing colour against colour, seeing the composition grow, combined with the conviction that all is going well, this is the joy of painting. Several hours of concentrated activity later, the time will come for a pause; tiredness or family demands will mean leaving the studio but in high spirits with the conviction that the work is going well.

In the cold light of morning the shock of seeing the product of the previous day's labours as flawed, banal, boring and bad undermines the confidence so foolishly felt on the previous day. Coming to terms with this disappointment, which could easily stop all further attempts to create a piece of work, was probably the most difficult part of the journey to become an artist. My way out of this dilemma was to attack the work with renewed energy until the battle was won, or I put the work on one side. Swinging from elation to despair and back to elation was exhausting, but I was trapped in the possibility of achieving a high, and my Ceredigion genes meant that I could not stop. Creating a piece of art is entirely mysterious, a process which requires faith and the acceptance of the need for repeated revision and adjustment of the initial motif. The following is my statement from 1985:

> I continue to paint because the application of each brush stroke holds the possibility of transformation. To have the ability to bring about change is important and gives hope. Repeated engagements with the resistant quality of paint brings about a transformation of the motif which can never be preconceived, and if the work goes well is always a surprise and is sometimes magical.

Anton Ehernzweig (*The Hidden Order of Art*) mentions Heinz Koppel, who talked about the beneficial conflict between the artist's point of departure and the resisting medium:

> A new idea will inevitably be modified through its impact on the resisting medium and conversely impose an entirely new use on the medium.

The passage of time is a factor that plays an important part in the process of creation and in the artist's understanding and response to what has been brought into existence through her engagement with the medium. Years of experience have taught me that at a certain point a piece of work will need to be left resting for days, weeks or even months. Returning to it one greets it as a stranger: who produced this surprising configuration? It is at this time, looking at it with a fresh eye, that what it needs for completion is understood in a flash.

The act of making art opens a gateway to the subconscious. Hours can pass whilst the artist is absorbed in a sequence of intuitive decisions. This is followed by further adjustments made using the critical faculties of the brain. Understanding the rhythmical movement between intuitive and rational thinking recognised as the functions of the right and left sides of the brain needs to be accepted as the foundation of creative activity. Developing a relationship with an inner voice, a relaxed acceptance of ideas that come from nowhere, and building a confidence in the importance of irrational decisions, is a step towards finding a personal voice:

> I am absolutely convinced that all decisions about colour are completely irrational. I think it belongs in that domain, it doesn't have to be reasonable.
>
> *Stanley William Hayter*

Colour

Orchestrating colour to create new and unexpected juxtapositions is central to the language that I have tried to bring into being. My heroes are the mostly anonymous makers of the Welsh quilt tradition; Paul Klee, and Matisse.

> One day I must be able to improvise freely on the keyboards of colours, the row of watercolours in my paint box.
>
> *Paul Klee*

It is my belief that colourists are born, but not made. As in the field of music it is said that some are blessed with perfect pitch. So in the use of colour a few artists have the mastery of tone, pitch and volume that enables them to explore complex unexpected colour relationships that are beyond the reach of average practitioners. 'Polyphony' is a term to describe music containing parts of equal significance which are played simultaneously. For Klee, polyphonic painting meant a layering of various structured areas producing many voices. The concept of layering combined with the exploration of colour echoes the direction of my present work.

Two visits to India in 1995 and 97 have enabled me to orchestrate my palette with more confidence and to extend my ambition with colour. India is important for me, as this was the first culture that I had experienced where everyone has a sophisticated understanding of how colours interact with each other. What a joy it was to see whole families, parents and two, three or four children, wearing garments that created a moving painting of extraordinary colour juxtapositions. Seeing these rainbow abstractions, I felt permitted to go further along the path set by Paul Klee.

In Rajasthan I was impressed by the way everyone seemed to follow an instinct to decorate and make patterns to embellish everything. Women decorated the doorways and walls of the home each year in honour of a particular festival. These decorations in ochre and chocolate-coloured earth on clay walls were joyful and bold. 'The artist is not a special kind of man, but man is a special kind of artist' (Anand Coomaraswamy). Discovering this statement was profoundly liberating, and in stark contrast to Western culture, where the cult of genius, and the concept that an artist is a being apart from the rest of society, is the source of many problems.

During my visits to India I was able to visit villages where the block printing of textiles was a thriving business in small family-run enterprises. Frames holding suspended walls of coloured cloth were for me a visual feast, as were fields laid out with patterned fabric, where women dressed in brilliant saris created a ballet as they walked amongst the cloth pieces, bending and moving as to a silent music.

My experience of seeing these textiles out in the fields, in the countryside, in the bright Indian light, confirmed my decision to link my work with the patchwork tradition that was part of my cultural background. The bold yet subtle patchworks in the collection of Jen Jones, owner of the Welsh Quilt Centre in Lampeter, are another dialect of the textile language. Appropriate that I should move in this direction, connecting my great-grandmother's quilt and my father and grandfathers' work spinning and weaving in *Y Ffatri* on the precipice above the Rheidol Valley.

A Visual Tradition

My search for a visual language within the culture of Wales led to my enthusiasm for archaeology.

As a painter my vocabulary is a collection of marks. These can be memories of hillsides, cloud shadows, leaves in the wind, or rock faces. To these I have added the spirals, zigzags and linear inventions of prehistoric carvings, which represent values that are in stark contrast to those of our global technological age. For me, the earliest art of Wales comes to us from prehistoric times. The mathematical skill and astronomical understanding of the builders of the monuments of *Barclodiad y Gawres* and *Bryn Celli Ddu* on Anglesey who could record the summer and winter solstices is truly awe-inspiring.

A search for a female perspective and a personal means of expression led to experiments with dyes on fabric. A wish to show a land under threat, to suggest the fragility of the natural order and to demonstrate a certain precariousness was my aim. Writing this at the time of the great floods in February 2014 shows an uncanny foresight, as I began experimenting with dyes in the early 80s. The marks produced when pouring dyes echo the organic forms that I see in the landscape. The discovery that I could paint with dyes was a breakthrough. Stitching, tearing, folding and quilting provide a fluid medium that serves as a link with women's historic work with textiles. In the face of trivialisation it is important to validate women's domestic labours and the craft traditions.

The national press and media daily feature articles on the lack of equality between the sexes that has barely been affected by the feminist movement which so inspired me in the 60s. Little has changed in Wales, where the male dominance inherited from the powerful Nonconformist tradition in chapel culture continues. This is my favourite line from a poem by Menna Elfyn: '*ac a wnaiff y gwragedd aros ar ôl*' (and will the wives stay behind). (In chapel culture men were community leaders, wives made the tea.)

The Historic Atlas of Ceredigion was published in 1955, one year before I left Cardiff College of Art. At the back of this book a list appears of famous names associated with Ceredigion, 185 of whom were men, but there is only one woman, Sara Jane Rees (or to give her her Bardic name, Cranogwen). This is dramatic confirmation that in the culture which was my background, women were invisible and their achievements unrecorded. Cranogwen (1839–1916) in fact ran a navigation school in Llangrannog, Ceredigion, was a poet, and started the first women's magazine in Wales.

Against this background of misogyny it is cheering to think of of a small nation like Finland where a much better balance of equality between men and women has been achieved. Here in Wales where much prejudice remains and the culture is still male dominated, nevertheless a few chinks have appeared in the barricades and a small number of women are managing to make a difference: Elin Jones, our energetic AM, and Ellen ap Gwynn, the new leader of Ceredigion County Council. Aberystwyth University in Dr April Mac Mahon has the first female Vice Chancellor of a Welsh University, and Ffion Hague has presented and researched an inspiring series of television films on historic Welsh women and their achievements. Leanne Wood is the leader of Plaid Cymru; we must remember the contributions of our poets, Menna Elfyn writing in Welsh and English, and Gwyneth Lewis and Gillian Clarke. These form a creative sisterhood that can sustain and encourage many more to achieve their potential.

There remains one other dragon to be slain on the path to finding a voice as an artist. It is necessary for an artist to be able to handle rejection. Working in any art form is to enter a competitive field. Female artists who decide to invade the male territory of fine art must expect a procession of rejections and exclusions. Lifting a head above the parapet will certainly result in being shot down. Being left out of anthologies of contemporary practitioners and excluded from group shows is common practice. It is at this point that a safety net must be created that will maintain confidence and preserve energy for future work. A safety net can be created by being surrounded by a body of work yet to be resolved but holding the hope of ambitions to be fulfilled. The artist needs to be cossetted and comforted by a treasure house of hopeful beginnings which can spark another creative journey. One day is the maximum time allowed to grieve over a rejection.

Over the years I have enjoyed many opportunities and I have also survived a long procession of rejections, which continue.

2009 was a good year for me, including being selected to be part of the 'Celebrating the Red Dragon Exhibition', which toured four cities in China. The three artists selected by Chinese curators were myself, Christine Mills and Iwan Bala. This was a new and unexpected experience for me and provided me with a most gratifying boost of confidence. The good times continued when in the same year I was invited to be part of the Wales Smithsonian Festival in Washington DC.

Over 100 practitioners from Wales took part in an across-the-art-forms celebration of creativity and talent which was the brainchild of First Minister Rhodri Morgan. The National Eisteddfod could learn much from the great success of the format adopted by this festival. Being commissioned to design the Wales banner for the Mall in Washington DC for the duration of the Festival brought with it a warm glow that I continue to treasure.

Aberystwyth: Art and Architecture

Although very familiar with Aberystwyth having attended Ardwyn Grammar School walking daily through the streets and up and down the promenade, after moving back to Aberystwyth in 2001 I could see and appreciate architectural details which I had missed in earlier years.

Aberystwyth town is in fact an architectural gem. Unlike many other places, Aberystwyth has maintained the character of its town centre with individual buildings of architectural merit interspersed with Victorian and Edwardian terraces. No motorway has been carved through the centre and so far we have been spared large-scale demolition. We can learn from France and Italy, where great pride and interest is taken in the design of the built environment, and the will is there to restore and preserve, as opposed to the rampant destruction which is such a characteristic of urban Britain.

To appreciate the rich variety of styles in the streets and terraces it is necessary to focus on details. The porches, doorways and windows of houses in Park Avenue, Alexandra Road, Stanley Terrace and Penglais Hill are a feast of exuberant invention.

Against a background of a rich built heritage, Aberystwyth has three outstanding public buildings: the Old College, the National Library and the Chemistry Building, which now houses the School of Art. I have ben blessed with the good fortune to have been given studio space in all three.

The nature of the space in a studio will determine to some extent the nature of the work produced in it. When my exhibition 'First Language' was being planned to be shown in the Gregynog Gallery of the National Library in 2006 building work was proceeding on the Drwm. For about two years I shared a corner of the Gregynog Gallery with a cement mixer and missing floorboards, whilst the work proceeded. The Gregynog Gallery is a splendid high-ceilinged panelled room filled with light, so painting there was a great privilege and allowed me to envisage how my work would occupy the space in my exhibition. Having access to the reading rooms and the expertise of the staff enabled me to produce digital works incorporating material from the Library collections, which I developed with artist Tom Piper and the V6 group of Artist Publishers in Cardiff. Having this period of close relationship with the National Library and its treasures was fundamental in the development of my ideas. Working in an inspirational building, in this case also in a spectacular location overlooking the town and the bay generated energy and optimism for the task of painting.

After that exhibition in 2006, I was welcomed the next year into the School of Art, where I was allowed to use one of the large studios whilst the students were away for the summer.

The School of Art occupies one of the finest examples of architecture in Aberystwyth. The Edward Davies Building celebrated its centenary in 2007. It is an elegant symbol of the schools aim to join the traditional and contemporary. It was the first purpose-built chemical laboratory in a British university, designed by Alfred W. S. Cross, a prize-winning architect opened in 2007 by Lord Asquith. The building cost of £23,000 was met in total by the David Davies family.

The School of Art, formerly the Visual Art Department, opened here in 1995. This building overlooking the town and Cardigan Bay, with its grand Wrenaissance-style facade incorporating two wings and a central cupola over a sweeping staircase, lends dignity and status to the activity housed within its walls. The polished staircase, black and white marble floor and highly-polished brass door fittings set the scene for walking into the large studio which, I maintain, is like walking into heaven. Bathed in light from the vast overhead windows this space provides the very best conditions for painting and photography. Being able to walk 44 feet away from the painting, and being able to have several works in the studio spread out to be seen together, are the best possible conditions for making work that sings.

The other establishment in Aberystwyth which has been especially supportive from the time it opened in 1972 is the Arts Centre. Before moving to Aberystwyth in 2001 I ran outreach programmes in Newcastle Emlyn and Dre Fach Felindre, and since 2001 I have been involved in running occasional one day workshops and Summer Courses. The education programme run by Aberystwyth Arts Centre is known for its excellence and breadth of activity beyond Wales. I have developed friendships with a large community of painters from all parts of Wales and beyond through this contact through workshops.

I was one of the first tenants of the creative units built amongst the trees behind the Arts Centre, which at night look as if a spaceship has landed. I moved out of my silver studio only when I was tempted by another opportunity.

The Old College

Realising that several post-graduate students from the School of Art had studios in the old College, and knowing at this point that the future of the building was uncertain, I enquired whether I could have a studio somewhere in this astonishing structure. The culmination of my ambition was reached when I moved up two flights of a spiral staircase to my new studio in January 2013.

The eccentric asymmetrical character of this building

that incorporates so much Welsh history embedded in its fabric is a nourishing environment for creativity. Walking through the quadrangle with its surprising balconies, openings, arches and noble staircases can be compared to walking into a painting or a stage set. The Old College contains a wealth of splendid large rooms, many overlooking the sea with large windows. All this at present is in a period of transition as various departments leave for the campus on Penglais Hill.

Professor Roger Webster wrote *Old College, Aberystwyth*, a comprehensive history of this extraordinary building which was published in 1995 by the University of Wales Press. Reading this book is recommended if you wish to understand and fully appreciate the story of this structure:

> Old College, Aberystwyth is a spectacular High Victorian building within which resides the ghost of an earlier house. This is Castle House built in the early 1790s by Uvedale Price as a holiday house for his wife Lady Caroline. In 1824 Castle house was sold. In 1864 the railway line from Machynlleth reached Aberystwyth and plans were made to convert Castle House into an Hotel. The architect employed for its conversion was John Pollard Seddon.

Perhaps this is the right time to appreciate the irrational character of the Gothic as demonstrated in the Old College. The decades of Brutalist concrete and Corbusier-led modernism has left a hunger for something different. The exuberance of the astonishing variety that goes into the many sections of this building and the way they are combined to create a unified whole gives me a daily reason to smile as I climb the two flights of spiral steps to my studio.

I am convinced that the spaces that we occupy have a profound effect on levels of energy and mental health. The magnificent quadrangle, with its asymmetrical doorways, windows and stairs, is unique. The organic nature of the building, decisions being made as the work proceeded, has given a joyful spontaneity to the features. Both William Morris and John Ruskin wrote of the importance they placed on a worker enjoying his tasks. We have inherited a building that expresses pleasure and delight in pattern and proportion. The creative decisions made can now be treasured and enjoyed, as a total contrast to acres of concrete and the sad state of much building from the 1960s and 70s.

Uvedale Price had been on a grand Tour of Europe and had published his *Essay on the Picturesque*. Price had views on what could be aesthetically pleasurable, which he wished to see expressed in Castle House. These were variety and intricacy, and the contrast of opposites, roughness and sudden variation joined to that of irregularity. These qualities were the most efficient causes of the picturesque. The foundation of what became the Old College was laid down by Uvedale Price, but these ideas were then incorporated by John Pollard Seddon, who became the architect mainly responsible for the building we see today. C. J. Ferguson was responsible for certain sections, which explains the unexpected contrasts of style which can be detected on close inspection of certain juxtapositions.

Castell Coch near Cardiff and Cardiff Castle, both built by Lord Bute and spectacular examples of Extreme Victorian Gothic Architecture, were designed by Augustus Pugin, who was a strong influence on John Seddon. Both of these buildings attract big visitor numbers and are celebrated as architectural masterpieces.

The Old College is also comparable with Strawberry Hill, the famous Gothic house built by Horace Walpole in 1749.

The potential benefits for Aberystwyth, west Wales, the whole of Wales, are incalculable when this much-loved building finds a new role as outlined in the Feasibility Study 2013 and opens its doors so that a new audience will be able to enjoy a unique piece of architecture filled with treasures that reflect the culture of Wales.

Important is the fact that this building is a monument to Welsh national identity, bought in 1872 with the pennies of the miners and quarrymen.

Seddon knew the Pre-Raphaelites, and was much influenced by John Ruskin and William Morris, so the architectural concepts explored by Seddon were the new ideas that became the Arts and Crafts movement, which had its beginnings in Britain but which eventually spread to Europe, USA and Canada. William Morris and John Ruskin were both concerned to keep alive the skills and dignity of work produced by hand when confronted with the changes brought about by mechanical production. The joy of experiencing the spaces to be explored in the Old College is the fact that this is a building that grew organically incorporating changes as required. William Morris maintained that artists need two teachers, nature and history. You do not find straight lines in nature. So in the Old College you will find spiral staircases, curves and circles, no endless corridors but corners and niches full of surprises. If you keep your eyes glued to your mobile or iPhone, details such as gargoyles embellishing the exterior of the building will be missed.

If you look at the plan of the building you will see that it follows the curve of the shore and takes on the shape of a boat. There is no back or front to this structure so the whole functions as a feast for the eyes, incorporating much variety and ornament yet maintaining a unity overall, as good pieces of art must do. The designer of the Old College borrowed ideas from medieval cathedrals.

John Seddon had an enthusiasm for all the visual arts; his brother was a painter, and he wished that all forms of visual expression should have the potential link with architecture. As I gaze down from the balcony outside my studio onto the quadrangle, I am comforted to see the bronze of Tom Ellis MP, an old student of the college, who raises his hand in greeting. In a lecture delivered to the Society of the Cymmrodorion on 10 March 1897 he called for the need for a National Gallery for Wales alongside a National Museum and National Library. His presence convinces me that it is appropriate to engage in the creation of art in this building.

Now, 107 years after Tom Ellis urged his fellow countrymen to embrace visual expression in the arts, a deficit persists in Wales of provision for developing an audience for visual culture. Wales has missed out on the growing appreciation for visual art. The public appetite for visiting galleries continues unabated, as is shown by the 7.4 million visitors to the four Tate Galleries in 2011.

The National Library and the National Museum all include the visual arts in their programme, but compared with literature and music the visual arts remain a poor relation.

Scotland and Ireland can provide a model of what is needed. In Scotland the visual arts are well established and visual artists are celebrated as National Treasures. All have heard of the Scottish colourists. Wales has colourists of equal achievement but apart from Ceri Richards they remain unrecognised. My list would include Roger Cecil, Catrin Webster, Sue Hunt, Catrin Williams, Glyn Baines, and Terry Setch. In Ireland, Kilmainham Hospital has been transformed from a military establishment during British rule into a splendid contemporary art gallery that gives status to visual culture and encourages pride in identity.

In Wales we have *Llên Cymru*/Literature Wales, a funded body that ensures that opportunities are created for writers, and we have a succession of National Poets. The Welsh National Opera is well housed and supported, as is the National Orchestra and National Dance company. There is also the Cardiff Singer of the World competition.

An opportunity presents itself now with the possibility of correcting this imbalance in Welsh culture by making sections of the Old College serve as a permanent home for Welsh visual culture. The Old College building could lend itself to many complementary cultural activities whilst allowing the visual arts a well-deserved exposure.

Today, artists of all disciplines, composers, dancers, photographers, film makers, painters and printmakers could be inspired by this astonishing building. An international artists' residency programme, on the lines of the Banff Centre in Canada and the Tyrone Guthrie Centre in Ireland, would invigorate Aberystwyth, make it a destination and confirm it as a cultural centre.

Tom Ellis had a strong voice advocating a more balanced provision for Welsh culture and he was not alone. Sir Cedric Morris, a member of the industrialist family that gave their name to the town of Morriston, was an accomplished and well-connected painter. Born in Swansea he spent much energy trying to improve the lot of Welsh artists. He ran an open studio in Suffolk, which Glyn Morgan from Pontypridd attended, and which provided a base for Heinz Koppel. He was associated with the vibrant arts centre in Merthyr Tudful run by Mary Horsfalls, and organised perhaps the first exhibition of Welsh Art in 1935.

One of my treasured possessions is a letter from Cedric Morris dated 1965 from Benton End in Hadleigh, Suffolk, telling me that he thought my paintings were the best in the Newtown National Eisteddfod; also that he would like to see more of my work. My ignorance was such that I had no idea who he was and never followed up his invitation to show him more of my work.

In the twenty-first century Wales needs another strong advocate for the importance of learning to see, to be able to read buildings, to be able to enjoy variety and pattern, all this can enrich everyone's life immeasurably. Man-made structures can be a feast for the eyes and some buildings have been described as music in stone. I quote here from Patrick Leigh Fermor's *A Time of Gifts*. This could be a description of the Old College:

> Overtures and preludes followed each other as courtyard opened upon courtyard. Ascending staircases unfolded as vaingloriously as pavanes. Cloisters developed with the complexity of double, triple and quadruple fugues. The suites of state departments concatenated with variety, the mood and décor of symphonic movements. A magnificent and measured polyphony crept in ones ears until everything vibrated with controlled and pervading splendour.

There is, I believe, a direct connection between the care and maintenance of our architectural heritage, the quality of new building, and the low status given to the visual arts in the culture of Wales. The toxic influence of the greed-promoting casino-banking culture spreads even to remote areas of mid Wales. The result is that the undemocratic and opaque system of planning is a recipe for the disasters that are unfolding. Aberystwyth continues to mourn the loss of the splendid Art Deco King's Hall on the promenade, and the Victorian town clock, both replaced by vastly inferior structures. Now in the twenty-first century we have a procession of eyesores marching down Park Avenue, the entrance to the town: hotels, council and Welsh Assembly offices soon to be joined by a department store complex of monumental banality. The enemy here is visual illiteracy, the lack of a visual tool kit which is about learning to see what you are looking at. Contrast this with Italy. In Italy, ordinary workmen and women, not architects or designers, appreciate the details of proportion, measurement and contrast of scale which is a feature of the architectural wealth to be found in all Italian towns.

Today all art forms are porous; ideas flow from music into colour into theatre. Welsh art, in order to fully contribute to the future potential of this cross-fertilisation, needs to proceed on a firm foundation, with the same respect and support awarded to, for example, literature. Llên Cymru/Literature Wales, housed in the Millennium Centre in Cardiff, is a body that supports and creates opportunities for writers. We have a rotating role of National Poet. An award that recognised achievement in the visual arts could bring about a change of culture.

As I have mentioned earlier, *Aosdána* (People of the Arts) is an Irish association of artists. It was created in 1981 to give support across all art forms. In 2007 the Scottish government announced the setting up of an arts group modelled on *Aosdána*. Arts practitioners in Wales should urge the Senedd to explore what might be learned here. Rhuthun Centre for Applied Arts, led by Philip Hughes, is a good role model for other galleries to follow, supporting art made in Wales and taking it beyond our border.

The Gas Gallery

At a time when current affairs, floods, the financial recession, youth unemployment and threatening events in the Ukraine and the Middle East blow clouds of negativity into deepest west Wales, the phenomenal amount of energy created by the launch of the artist-led project Oriel Nwy/Gas Gallery is something to reassure and to celebrate.

In November 2012 the artists' group Celf Ceredigion Art secured a licence to run a gallery in what had originally been a gas showroom, and subsequently became the Bangor Garage car and motorbike showroom on Park Avenue, Aberystwyth. The licence was granted by Ceredigion County Council, owner of the building in question. Following the success of the project in its first nine months, the licence was extended for another year, with the possibility of a third year, depending on the circumstances.

Already over 100 artists have taken part in the main exhibition programme. And this has grown organically into regular and spontaneous performances by musicians and storytellers, and various multi-media explorations. It is remarkable that the whole enterprise runs on the energy of volunteers. Almost fifty volunteers are involved in the day-to-day running of the space, including students from the university. It is obvious that the artists who have contributed the hours, skills and materials, sanding floors, hanging work, painting walls, have done this because they know the value of having a gallery, and that the potential of socialising with kindred spirits will benefit them as creative practitioners.

The Gas Gallery is important because it provides a window to show primarily the work of artists living in Ceredigion. The difference between this project and the programmes of publicly-funded galleries is that the funded galleries will mainly show work that has been curated elsewhere. A small proportion of exhibitions will show the work of Wales-based artists, but imported exhibitions often reinforce the idea that acceptable art is produced elsewhere. In the short history of the gallery, a pattern is already emerging across art forms. The geology and history of Ceredigion is reflected in the work of several of the artists – for example, a focus on the lead-mining remains has resulted in sculptures, paintings, constructions and storytelling. Over 5,000 visitors have already been to the gallery. Openings attract as many as 200 enthusiasts, and the response to all the exhibitions has created an extraordinary spark of vitality in the community of artists spilling over into the rest of the population. Aberystwyth could achieve its potential as a destination for those who value the arts and who would appreciate the undoubted buzz emanating from the Gas Gallery if this project were to be given the necessary funding support in order to develop. The enthusiasm of the community has already been demonstrated, and I can envisage the Gas Gallery, to the east of the town, working in tandem with the developments planned for the Old College, to the west. The Gas Gallery has the massive advantage of large windows, making the work and activity accessible from the street and visible to passing traffic.

Behind the gallery is a sheltered yard, in which a shed built to house a motorbike repair shop has been taken over by Richard Brown, a sculptor in slate and other materials, and Aberystwyth Printmakers, who are running evening and weekend courses in lithography, etching, block printing and screen printing. Aberystwyth Printmakers is a vibrant organisation, with a membership of over fifty, mainly from Ceredigion but also from further afield. They celebrate their first decade in 2014 with an exhibition at the Museum of Modern Art (MOMA), the Tabernacl, Machynlleth.

Aberystwyth Printmakers flourishes because of the status and excellence of the membership, who represent the most able and talented artists in west Wales. The leading artist in this organisation is Paul Croft, an exceptionally gifted artist and craftsman, who trained as a master printmaker in the Tamarind Institute of Lithography in Albuquerque, New Mexico. Paul's reputation and international standing attracts students and membership, and undoubtedly given some support and recognition further development would be possible, making Aberystwyth an international centre for printmaking, and bringing great benefits for the town and the area.

History does not repeat itself, but echoes of past events can sometimes indicate the way forward. Many individuals who have enriched and changed Welsh visual culture in the last three decades were involved in the short-lived multidisciplinary phenomenon known as the Barn Centre/Y Sgubor, in Aberystwyth in the 1980s. We know and value the work of the theatre company 'Brith Gof', and of Cliff McLucas, Mike Pearson, Liz Jones, Keith Morris, Peter Lord, Marian Delyth, and so many more. The vibrations emanating from the Gas Gallery and Aberystwyth Printmakers, and the possibilities of awakening the Old College to a new life, might indicate something blowing in the wind.

Artists cannot function in a vacuum. Artists need the community of other artists and a wider supportive culture if great art is to be a possibility.

Oriel Nwy/Gas Gallery is perhaps the first green shoot of a flowering of all the arts in Aberystwyth, following the pattern set in other remote locations, such as the Pier Arts Centre, Stromness, Orkney, and the Tate St Ives in Cornwall.

Afterword

Art cannot exist unless a working communication can be reached, and this communication is an activity in which both artist and spectator participate, Below this activity threshold there can be no art.

The special nature of the artist's work is his use of a learned skill in a particular kind of transmission of experience. The traditional meaning of 'art' was precisely 'skill'. The transmission of valued experience, the felt importance of his experience.

The struggle to remake ourselves, to change our personal organisation so that we may live in a proper relationship to our environment, is in fact often painful. To think of making contact with others, rather than of making contact with this precise experience, is irrelevant and distracting.

The artist's way of remaking himself is as in man generally by work, which is remaking the environment and in learning to work, remaking himself. The art work has been made and the artist has remade himself in a continuous process.

It is neither subject working on object, nor object on subject; it is rather a dynamic interaction, which is in fact a whole and continuous process.

It is often through art that the society expresses its sense of being a society. The Artist, in this case, is not the lonely explorer, but the voice of his/her community.

The Artist in such a case, is not simply copying the common meanings, the meanings are his own in deep realisation, yet the conditions for their communication are powerfully available. Successful communication depends on the organisation of audiences as well as artists.

Communication is the process of making unique experience into common experience and it is above all the claim to live.

Sharing of common meanings, and thence common activities and purposes, reception and comparison of new meanings leading to the tensions and achievements of growth and change.

Raymond Williams

References and Further Reading

Page 31   Dumfrieshire to Eisteddfa Gurig. Story from family archive
          of Gwynn Lewis, Erwbarfe Ponterwyd (uncle)
Page 34   Dafydd Jones, Master Ship builder. This information taken
          from an article by the late Gareth Owen in *Country Quest*
          Volume V1 No.2 Autumn 1965 p.20
Page 38   *Clych Atgof,* publisher Cwmni Cyhoeddwyr Cymreig (cyf.)
          Caernarfon 1906
Page 45   *Anglo Welsh Review,* Spring 1972
Page 70   Barbara Hepworth. *Some statements* by Barbara Hepworth,
          Barbara Hepworth Museum, St Ives, Cornwall 1977
Page 78   David Jones, *Epoch and Artist,* Faber and Faber, London
          1959
Page 91   *The Artist in Wales,* David Bell 1957
Page 91   *The Grammer of Ornament,* Owen Jones
Page 91   *The Aesthetics of Relevance* by Peter Lord, Gwasg Gomer,
          Changing Wales series. 1992
Page 92   John Ruskin, *The Stones of Venice,* first published 1853
          (paperback Da Capo)
Page 94   *Survival* by Margaret Atwood, Anansi Press, Toronto 1992
Page 99   *The Hidden Order of Art* by Anton Eherenzweig, Weidenfeld
          and Nicholson 1967
Page 100 Paul Klee, *Painting Music,* publisher Prestel/ Munich/
          London/ New York
Page 104 Menna Elfyn, *Aderyn Bach Mewn Llaw,* Gwasg Gomer 1990
Page 104 *A Historic Atlas of Ceredigion* by W. J. Lewis MSc, Cyngor Sir
          Ceredigion 1955
Page 110 *The Old College, Aberystwyth* by Roger Webster, University
          of Wales Press, Cardiff 1995
Page 113 *Speeches and Addresses of Tom Ellis MP,* publisher Hughes
          and Son, Wrexham 1012
Page 115 *A Time of Gifts* by Patrick Leigh Fermore
Page 121 *The Long Revolution,* Raymond Williams. First published by
          Chatto and Windus 1961, Pelican books 1965. Quotations
          from part one 'The Creative Mind'.

Further reading:

The Celtic Twilight, WB Yates first published in 1981 by Colin Smythe Limited, Gerards Cross, England

The Master and his Emissary. The Divided Brain and the Making of the Western World by Iain McGilchrist, Yale University Press, 2010